TRELAWNY OF THE "WELLS"

An Original Comedietta in Four Acts

BY

ARTHUR W. PINERO

LONDON
NEW YORK SYDNEY TORONTO HOLLYWOOD

ISBN 0 573 01459 0

Please see page iv for further copyright information

TRELAWNY OF THE "WELLS"

Played for the first time at the Court Theatre, London, on January 20th, 1898.

THE PERSONS OF THE PLAY

Theatrical Folk

JAMES TELFER	(of the Bagnigge-Wells Theatre).	*Mr. Athol Forde.*
AUGUSTUS COLPOYS		*Mr. E. M. Robson.*
FERDINAND GADD		*Mr. G. du Maurier.*
TOM WRENCH		*Mr. Paul Arthur.*
MRS. TELFER (MISS VIOLET SYLVESTER)		*Mrs. E. Saker.*
AVONIA BUNN		*Miss Pattie Browne.*
ROSE TRELAWNY		*Miss Irene Vanbrugh.*
IMOGEN PARROTT (of the Royal Olympic Theatre)		*Miss Hilda Spong.*
O'DWYER (Prompter at the Pantheon Theatre) .		*Mr. Richard Purdon.*
MEMBERS OF THE COMPANY OF THE PANTHEON THEATRE		*Mr. Vernon, Mr. Foster, Mr. Mellon and Miss Baird.*
HALL-KEEPER AT THE PANTHEON		*Mr. W. H. Quinton.*

Non-theatrical Folk

VICE-CHANCELLOR SIR WILLIAM GOWER, KNT. .		*Mr. Dion Boucicault.*
ARTHUR GOWER	(his Grandchildren) . . .	*Mr. James Erskine.*
CLARA DE FŒNIX		*Miss Eva Williams.*
MISS TRAFALGAR GOWER (Sir William's Sister) .		*Miss Isabel Bateman.*
CAPTAIN DE FŒNIX (Clara's Husband) . . .		*Mr. Sam Sothern.*
MRS. MOSSOP		*Miss Le Thière.*
MR. ABLETT		*Mr. Fred Thorne.*
CHARLES		*Mr. Aubrey Fitzgerald.*
SARAH		*Miss Polly Emery.*

COPYRIGHT INFORMATION

(See also page ii)

SCENE PLOT

ACT I

Mr. and Mrs. Telfer's Lodgings at No. 2, Brydon Crescent, Clerkenwell. May.

ACT II

At Sir William Gower's, in Cavendish Square. June.

ACT III

Again in Brydon Crescent. December.

ACT IV

On the Stage of the Pantheon Theatre a few days later.

Period.—Somewhere in the early 'sixties.

Note.—Bagnigge (locally pronounced, Bagnidge) Wells—formerly a popular mineral spring in Islington, London, situated not far from the better remembered Sadler's-Wells. The gardens of Bagnigge-Wells were at one time much resorted to; but, as a matter of fact, Bagnigge-Wells, unlike Sadler's-Wells, has never possessed a playhouse. Sadler's-Wells Theatre, however—always familiarly known as the "Wells"—still exists. It was rebuilt in 1876–7.

A DIRECTION TO THE STAGE MANAGER

The costumes and scenic decoration of this little play should follow, to the closest detail, the mode of the early 'sixties—the period, in dress, of crinoline and the peg-top trouser; in furniture, of horsehair and mahogany, and the abominable "walnut-and-rep." No attempt should be made to modify such fashions in illustration, to render them less strange, even less grotesque, to the modern eye. On the contrary, there should be an endeavour to reproduce, perhaps to accentuate, any feature which may now seem particularly quaint and bizarre. Thus, lovely youth should be shown decked uncompromisingly as it was at the time indicated, at the risk (which the author believes to be a slight one) of pointing the chastening moral that, while beauty fades assuredly in its own time, it may appear to succeeding generations not to have been beauty at all.

NOTE

On the occasion of the revival at the Old Vic I struck out all mention of Bagnigge-Wells from the programme and frankly described the Company of the "Wells" as "of Sadler's-Wells Theatre." Also, in Act I, I further gave up disguise by making Mrs. Mossop speak of Rose Trelawny as "the best juvenile-lady the 'Wells' has known since Mr. Phelps's management."

A. P.

TRELAWNY OF THE "WELLS"

ACT I

The SCENE *represents a sitting-room on the first floor of a respectable lodging-house. On the* R. *are two sash-windows, made to open, having Venetian blinds and giving a view of houses on the other side of the street. At the back, in the* C. *of the stage, is a fireplace. The grate is hidden by an ornament composed of shavings and paper roses. Over the fireplace is a mirror, and on each side of the fireplace a sideboard-cupboard. Down* L. *there is a door opening on to the stage; a landing is seen outside.* R., *between the windows, stand a cottage piano and a piano-stool. On the wall, above the piano, hangs a small looking-glass. Before each window there is a chair, and on the* R. *and* L. *of the fireplace an armchair. Against the wall* L., *just above the door, is a sofa. Above the sofa stands a large black trunk, the lid bulging with its contents and displaying some soiled theatrical finery. On the front of the trunk, in faded lettering, appear the words "Miss Violet Sylvester, Theatre Royal, Drury Lane." Under the sofa there are two or three pairs of ladies' satin shoes, much the worse for wear, and on the sofa a white-satin bodice, yellow with age, a heap of dog-eared playbooks, and some other litter of a like character. On the top of the piano there is some music, wax fruit under glass, a wig-block with a man's iron-grey ringlet-wig upon it, and in the corners of the room there stand some walking-sticks and a few theatrical swords. In the* C. *of the stage is a large circular table. There is a clean cover upon it, and on the top of the sideboard-cupboards are knives and forks, with black handles, plate, glass, cruet-stands, and some gaudy flowers in vases—all suggesting preparations for festivity.*

The woodwork of the room is grained, the ceiling plainly white-washed, and the wallpaper is of a neutral tint and much faded. The pictures are engravings in maple frames, and a portrait or two, in oil, framed in gilt. The furniture, curtains, and carpet are worn, but everything is clean and well kept.

The door is open throughout the act. The light is that of afternoon in early summer.

MRS. MOSSOP—*a portly, middle-aged Jewish lady, elaborately attired—is* L. *of the table laying the tablecloth.* ABLETT *enters hastily* L., *divesting himself of his coat as he does so. He is dressed in rusty black for "waiting."*

MRS. MOSSOP (*in a fluster*). Oh, here you are, Mr. Ablett——!

ABLETT. Good day, Mrs. Mossop. (*He crosses in front of table to up* R.)

MRS. MOSSOP (*bringing the cruet-stands from up* L.). I declare I thought you'd forgotten me.

ABLETT (*hanging his coat upon a curtain-knob up* R., *and turning up his shirt-sleeves*). I'd begun to fear I should never escape from the shop, ma'am. Jest as I was preparin' to clean myself, the 'ole universe seemed to cry aloud for pertaters. (*Relieving* MRS. MOSSOP *of the cruet-stands, and satisfying himself as to the contents of the various bottles.*) Now, you take a seat, Mrs. Mossop. You 'ave but to say "Mr. Ablett, lay for so many," and the exact number shall be laid for.

MRS. MOSSOP (*sinking into the armchair up* L.C.). I hope the affliction of short breath may be spared you, Ablett. Ten is the number.

ABLETT (*up* R.C., *whipping-up the mustard energetically*). Short-breathed you may be, ma'am, but not short-sighted. That gal of yours is no ordinary gal, but to 'ave set 'er to wait on ten persons would 'ave been to 'ave caught disaster. (*Glancing round the room.*) I am in Mr. and Mrs. Telfer's setting-room, I believe, ma'am?

MRS. MOSSOP (*turning in the chair and surveying the apartment complacently*). And what a handsomely proportioned room it is, to be sure!

ABLETT (*placing cruets* R.C. *and* L.C. *on the table*). May I h'ask if I am to 'ave the honour of includin' my triflin' fee for this job in their weekly book?

MRS. MOSSOP. No, Ablett—a separate bill, please.

(ABLETT *goes up* R. *and gets salt-cellars, then sees that they are right.*)

The Telfers kindly give the use of their apartment, to save the cost of holding the ceremony at the "Clown" Tavern; but share and share alike over the expenses is to be the order of the day.

ABLETT. I thank you, ma'am. (*Rubbing up the knives with a napkin.*) You let fall the word "ceremony," ma'am——

MRS. MOSSOP. Ah, Ablett, and a sad one—a farewell cold collation to Miss Trelawny.

ABLETT. Lor' bless me! I 'eard a rumour——

MRS. MOSSOP. A true rumour. She's taking her leave of us, the dear.

ABLETT (*putting two salt-cellars on table, one down stage, the other up stage*). This will be a blow to the "Wells," ma'am.

MRS. MOSSOP. The best juvenile-lady the "Wells" has known since Mr. Phelps's management.

ABLETT (*coming round front of table to* L. *of it and putting down the other two salt-cellars*). Report 'as it, a love affair, ma'am.

MRS. MOSSOP. A love affair, indeed! And a poem into the bargain, Ablett, if poet was at hand to write it.

Ablett. Reelly, Mrs. Mossop! (*He crosses above table to up* R., *takes up the two large beer-jugs, and turns to her.*) Is the beer to be bottled or draught, ma'am, on this occasion?

Mrs. Mossop. Draught for Miss Trelawny, invariably.

Ablett (*putting jugs at top of table*). Then draught it must be all round, out of compliment. Jest fancy! nevermore to 'ear customers speak of Trelawny of the "Wells," except as a pleasin' memory! A non-professional gentleman they give out, ma'am. (*He goes up for glasses.*)

Mrs. Mossop. Yes.

Ablett. Name of Glover. (*He brings glasses down* R. *of table.*)

Mrs. Mossop. Gower. Grandson of Vice-Chancellor Sir William Gower, Mr. Ablett.

Ablett (*polishing glasses*). You don't say, ma'am!

Mrs. Mossop (*rising*). No father nor mother, and lives in Cavendish Square with the old judge and a great aunt. (*She goes up* L. *for pickles.*)

Ablett. Then Miss Trelawny quits the Profession, ma'am, for good and all, I presoom?

Mrs. Mossop. Yes, Ablett. (*Putting pickles on table.*) She played last night for the last time—the last time on any stage.

(*She goes to the sideboard-cupboard up* L. *and brings the flowers to the table and arranges them, while* Ablett *sets out the knives and forks and two glasses.*)

Ablett. And when is the weddin' to be, ma'am?

Mrs. Mossop. It's not yet decided, Mr. Ablett. In point of fact, before the Gower family positively say Yes to the union, Miss Trelawny is to make her home in Cavendish Square for a short term—"short term" is the Gower family's own expression—in order to habituate herself to the West End.

(*She works round top of table to up* R. *of it.* Ablett *at the same time works round front of it to* L., *laying knives, forks, spoons, etc.*)

They're sending their carriage for her at two o'clock this afternoon, Mr. Ablett—their carriage and pair of bay horses.

Ablett. Well, I dessay a West End life has sooperior advantages over the Profession in some respecks, Mrs. Mossop.

Mrs. Mossop. When accompanied by wealth, Mr. Ablett. Here's Miss Trelawny but nineteen, and in a month-or-two's time she'll be ordering about her own powdered footman, and playing on her grand piano. How many actresses do *that*, I should like to know!

(Tom Wrench's *voice is heard.*)

Tom (*outside the door*). Rebecca! Rebecca, my loved one!

Mrs. Mossop (*down* R.C.). Oh, go along with you, Mr. Wrench!

(TOM *enters, with a pair of scissors in his hand. He is a shabbily dressed, ungraceful man of about thirty, with a clean-shaven face, curly hair, and eyes full of good-humour.*)

TOM. My own, especial Rebecca!

MRS. MOSSOP. Don't be a fool, Mr. Wrench! Now, I've no time to waste. I know you want something——

TOM (*moving below the table to* R). Everything, adorable. But most desperately do I stand in need of a little skilful trimming at your fair hands.

MRS. MOSSOP (*taking the scissors from him, coming down* R. *and clipping the frayed edges of his shirt-cuffs and collar*). First it's patching a coat, and then it's binding an Inverness——! Sometimes I wish that top room of mine was empty.

TOM. And sometimes I wish my heart was empty, cruel Rebecca.

MRS. MOSSOP (*giving him a thump*). Now, I really will tell Mossop of you, when he comes home! (*She turns* TOM *round to trim the back of his collar.*) I've often threatened it——

TOM (*to* ABLETT, *who is laying table,* L. *of it*). Whom do I see! No—it can't be—but yes—I believe I have the privilege of addressing Mr. Ablett, the eminent greengrocer, of Rosoman Street?

ABLETT (*sulkily*). Well, Mr. Wrench, and wot of it?

TOM. You possess a cart, good Ablett, which may be hired by persons of character and responsibility. "By the hour or job"—so runs the legend. I will charter it, one of these Sundays, for a drive to Epping.

ABLETT (L. *of table*). I dunno so much about that, Mr. Wrench.

TOM. Look to the springs, good Ablett, for this comely lady will be my companion.

MRS. MOSSOP. Dooce take your impudence! Give me your other hand. Haven't you been to rehearsal this morning with the rest of 'em?

TOM. I have, and have left my companions still toiling.

(ABLETT *works at back of table to* R. *of it.*)

My share in the interpretation of Sheridan Knowles's immortal work did not necessitate my remaining after the first act.

MRS. MOSSOP. Another poor part, I suppose, Mr. Wrench?

TOM. Another, and to-morrow yet another, and on Saturday two others—all equally, damnably rotten.

MRS. MOSSOP (*consolingly*). Ah, well, well! *somebody* must play the bad parts in this world, on and off the stage. There, (*returning the scissors*) there's no more edge left to fray; we've come to the soft. (*As he points the scissors at his breast.*) Ah! don't do that!

TOM. You are right, sweet Mossop. I won't perish on an empty stomach. (*Taking her aside to* L.) But tell me, shall I disgrace the feast, eh? Is my appearance too scandalously seedy?

MRS. MOSSOP. Not *it*, my dear.

Tom (*lovingly*). Miss Trelawny—do you think she'll regard me as a blot on the banquet? (*Wistfully.*) Do you, Beccy?

Mrs. Mossop. She! la! don't distress yourself. She'll be too excited to notice *you.*

Tom. H'm, yes! Now I recollect, she has always been that. Thanks, Beccy.

(*A knock, at the front door, is heard off stage* R. Mrs. Mossop *hurries to the window.*)

Mrs. Mossop. Who's that? (*Opening the lower window and looking out.*) It's Miss Parrott! Miss Parrott's arrived! (*She shuts window, and starts to cross towards* L.)

Tom. Jenny Parrott? Has Jenny condescended——?

Mrs. Mossop. *Jenny!* (*Passing him.*) Where are your manners, Mr. Wrench?

Tom (*grandiloquently*). Miss Imogen Parrott, of the Olympic Theatre. (*He gets to* R.C.)

Mrs. Mossop (*at the door, to* Ablett). Put your coat on, Ablett.

(Tom *puts scissors on piano* R.)

We are not selling cabbages.

(*She disappears, and is heard speaking in the distance.*)

Step up, Miss Parrott! Tell Miss Parrott to mind that mat, Sarah——!

Tom (*by piano*). Be quick, Ablett, be quick! The *élite* is below! More despatch, good Ablett!

Ablett (*above the table* C., *struggling into his coat—to* Tom, *spitefully*). Miss Trelawny's leavin' will make all the difference to the old "Wells." The season'll terminate abrupt, and then the comp'ny'll be h'out, Mr. Wrench—h'out, sir! (*He produces gloves and puts on the left one.*)

Tom (*adjusting his necktie, at the mirror over the piano*). Which will lighten the demand for the spongy turnip and the watery marrow, my poor Ablett.

Ablett (*under his breath*). Presumpshus! (*He gets* C., *then makes a horrifying discovery.*) Two lefts! That's Mrs. Ablett all over!

(*During the rest of the act, he is continually in difficulties, through his efforts to wear one of the gloves upon his right hand.* Mrs. Mossop *now re-enters, with* Imogen Parrott. Imogen *is a pretty, light-hearted young woman, of about seven-and-twenty, daintily dressed and carrying a parcel.*)

Mrs. Mossop (*outside, to* Imogen). There, it might be only yesterday you lodged in my house, (*she enters the room and gets* L.C., *up by the table*) to see you gliding up those stairs! And this the very room you shared with poor Miss Brooker——!

IMOGEN (*advancing to* TOM, *who is* R.C.). Well, Wrench, and how are you?

TOM (*bringing her a chair from front of window* R., *and demonstratively dusting the seat of it with his pocket-handkerchief*). Thank you, much the same as when you used to call me Tom.

IMOGEN. Oh, but I have turned over a new leaf, you know, since I have been at the Olympic.

MRS. MOSSOP. I am sure my chairs don't require dusting, Mr. Wrench.

TOM (*placing the chair* C., *below the table, and blowing his nose with his handkerchief, with a flourish*). My way of showing homage, Mossop.

MRS. MOSSOP. Miss Parrott has sat on them often enough, when she was an honoured member of the "Wells"—haven't you, Miss Parrott?

IMOGEN (*sitting* C., *with playful dignity*). I suppose I must have done so. Don't remind me of it.

(MRS. MOSSOP *gets near door.*)

I sit on nothing nowadays but down pillows covered with cloth of gold.

(MRS. MOSSOP *and* ABLETT *prepare to withdraw.* TOM *crosses up to fireplace.*)

MRS. MOSSOP (*at the door, to* IMOGEN). Ha, ha! la! I could fancy I'm looking at Und*i*ne again—Und*i*ne, the Spirit of the Waters.

(ABLETT *comes down* L.C. *with the two beer-jugs, gazing at* IMOGEN.)

She's not the least changed since she appeared as Und*i*ne—is she, Mr. Ablett?

ABLETT (*joining* MRS. MOSSOP). No—or as Prince Cammyralzyman in the pantomine. *I* never 'ope to see a pair o' prettier limbs ——

MRS. MOSSOP (*sharply*). Now then!

(*She pushes him out; they disappear.* TOM *moves down* L.C.)

IMOGEN (*after a shiver at* ABLETT'S *remark*). In my present exalted station I don't hear much of what goes on at the "Wells," Wrench. Are your abilities still—still——?

TOM (*on her* L.). Still unrecognized, still confined within the almost boundless and yet repressive limits of Utility—General Utility? (*Nodding.*) H'm, still.

IMOGEN. Dear me! a thousand pities! I positively mean it.

TOM. Thanks.

IMOGEN. What do you think! You were mixed up in a funny dream I dreamt one night lately.

TOM (*bowing*). Highly complimented.

IMOGEN. It was after a supper which rather—well, I'd had some strawberries sent me from Hertfordshire.

TOM. Indigestion levels all ranks.

IMOGEN. It was a nightmare. I found myself on the stage of the Olympic in that wig you—(*faint at the remembrance*) oh, gracious! You used to play your very serious little parts in it——

TOM. The wig with the ringlets?

IMOGEN. Ugh! yes.

TOM. I wear it to-night, for the second time this week, in a part which is very serious—and very little.

IMOGEN. Heavens! it *is* in existence then!

TOM. And long will be, I hope. (*A slight pause.*) I've only three wigs, and this one accommodates itself to so many periods.

IMOGEN. Oh, how it used to amuse the gallery-boys!

TOM. They still enjoy it. If you looked in this evening at half-past seven—I'm done at a quarter to eight—if you looked in at half-past seven, you would hear the same glad, rapturous murmur in the gallery when the presence of that wig is discovered. Not that they fail to laugh at my other wigs, at every article of adornment I possess, in fact! Good God, Jenny——!

IMOGEN (*wincing*). Ssssh!

TOM. Miss Parrott—if they gave up laughing at me now, I believe I—I believe I should—*miss it.* I believe I couldn't spout my few lines now in silence; my unaccompanied voice would sound so strange to me. Besides, I often think those gallery-boys are really fond of me, at heart. You can't laugh as they do—rock with laughter sometimes!—at what you dislike.

IMOGEN (*with sincerity*). Of course not. *Of course* they like you, Wrench. You cheer them, make their lives happier——

TOM (*walking about*). And to-night, by-the-by, I also assume that beast of a felt hat—the grey hat with the broad brim, and the imitation wool feathers. (*He crosses up* L., *then turns to her.*) You remember it?

IMOGEN. Y-y-yes.

TOM. I see you do. Well, that hat still persists in falling off, when I most wish it to stick on. It will tilt and tumble to-night—during one of Telfer's pet speeches; I feel it will.

IMOGEN. Ha, ha, ha!

TOM. And those yellow boots; I wear *them* to-night——

IMOGEN. No!

TOM. Yes!

IMOGEN. Ho, ho, ho, ho!

TOM (*with forced hilarity*). Ho, ho! ha, ha! And the spurs—the spurs that once tore your satin petticoat! You recollect——?

IMOGEN (*her mirth suddenly checked*). Recollect!

TOM. You would see those spurs to-night too, if you patronized us—*and* the red-worsted tights. The worsted tights are a little thinner, a little more faded and discoloured, a little more darned——

Oh, yes, thank you, I am still, as you put it, still—still—still——
(*He walks away, going to the mantelpiece and turning his back upon her.*)

IMOGEN (*after a brief pause*). I'm sure I didn't intend to hurt your feelings, Wrench.

TOM (*turning with some violence and coming down a step or two* L.C.). You! you hurt my feelings! Nobody can hurt my feelings! I have no feelings——!

(IMOGEN *starts up and, going to piano, puts her parasol upon it. Then she looks into mirror.* ABLETT *re-enters, carrying three chairs of odd patterns.* TOM *seizes two of the chairs and places them* R. *of the table, noisily.*)

ABLETT (*put out*). Look here, Mr. Wrench! if I'm to be 'ampered in performin' my dooties—— (*He places the remaining chair below the table.*)

TOM. More chairs, Ablett! In my apartment, the chamber nearest heaven, you will find one with a loose leg. We will seat Mrs. Telfer upon that. She dislikes me, and she is, in every sense, a heavy woman.

ABLETT (*moving towards the door—dropping his glove*). My opinion, you are meanin' to 'arrass me, Mr. Wrench——

TOM (*picking up the glove, and throwing it to* ABLETT*—singing*). "Take back thy glove, thou faithless fair!" Your glove, Ablett.

ABLETT. Thank you, sir, it *is* my glove and you are no gentleman.

(*He withdraws.* IMOGEN *crosses down to below the table.*)

TOM (*on* IMOGEN'S L.). True, Ablett—not even a Walking Gentleman.

IMOGEN. Don't go on so, Wrench. What about your plays? Aren't you trying to write any plays just now?

TOM. Trying! I am doing more than trying to write plays. I am writing plays. I have written plays.

(*They are both below the table.*)

IMOGEN. Well?

TOM. My cupboard upstairs is choked with 'em.

IMOGEN. Won't anyone take a fancy——?

TOM. Not a sufficiently violent fancy.

IMOGEN. You know, the speeches were so short, and had such ordinary words in them, in the plays you used to read to me—no big opportunity for the leading lady, Wrench.

TOM. M' yes. I strive to make my people talk and behave like live people, don't I——?

IMOGEN (*vaguely*). I suppose you do.

TOM. To fashion heroes out of actual, dull, everyday men—the sort of men you see smoking cheroots in the club windows in St.

James's Street; and heroines from simple maidens in muslin frocks. Naturally, the managers won't stand that.

IMOGEN. Why, of course not.

TOM. If *they* did, the public wouldn't.

IMOGEN. Is it likely?

TOM. Is it likely? I wonder!

IMOGEN. Wonder—what?

TOM. Whether they would.

IMOGEN. The public!

TOM. The public. Jenny, I wonder about it sometimes so hard that that little bedroom of mine becomes a banqueting-hall, and this lodging-house a castle.

(*There is a loud and prolonged knocking at the front door off* R.)

IMOGEN. Here they are, I suppose. (*She walks up* R. *a little, looking at her dress.*)

TOM (*pulling himself together*). Good lord! have I become dishevelled? (*He goes up as if to look in glass up* C.)

IMOGEN (*slyly*). Why, are you anxious to make an impression, even down to the last, Wrench?

(TOM *stops suddenly* L.C., *and leans over the table.*)

TOM (*angrily*). Stop that!

IMOGEN. It's no good your being sweet on her any longer, surely?

TOM (*glaring at her*). What cats you all are, you girls!

IMOGEN (R., *holding up her hands*). Oh! oh, dear! How vulgar —after the Olympic!

(ABLETT *returns, carrying three more chairs.*)

ABLETT (*arranging these chairs on the* L. *of the table, down stage*). They're all 'ome! they're all 'ome!

(TOM *withdraws, up the stage, and places the four chairs belonging to the room at the table.*)

(*To* IMOGEN.) She looks 'eavenly, Miss Trelawny does. I was jest takin' in the ale when she floated down the Crescent on her lover's arm. (*He comes down to front of table. Wagging his head at* IMOGEN *admiringly.*) There, I don't know which of you two is the——

IMOGEN (*haughtily*). Man, keep your place!

ABLETT (*hurt*). H'as you please, miss—but you apperently forget I used to serve you with vegetables.

(*He takes up a position at the door as* TELFER *and* GADD *enter.* TELFER *is a thick-set, elderly man, with a worn, clean-shaven face, and iron-grey hair "clubbed" in the theatrical fashion of the time. Sonorous, if somewhat husky, in speech, and elaborately dignified in bearing, he is at the same time a little uncertain about his H's.*

He has a tall hat on. GADD *is a flashily dressed young man of seven-and-twenty, with brown hair arranged à la Byron, and moustache of a deeper tone. He has a smoking-cap on.)*

TELFER (*advancing to* IMOGEN, *and kissing her, paternally*). Ha, my dear child! I heard you were 'ere. (*Kiss.*) Kind of you to visit us. Welcome! I'll just put my 'at down—— (*He places his hat on the top of the piano, and goes up the stage, inspecting the table.*)

GADD (*coming to* IMOGEN, *in an elegant, languishing way*). Imogen, my darling. (*Kissing her.*) Kiss Ferdy!

(*She kisses his cheek.*)

IMOGEN. Well, Gadd, how goes it?—I mean how are you?

GADD (*earnestly*). I'm hitting them hard this season, my darling. To-night, Sir Thomas Clifford. They're simply waiting for my Clifford.

IMOGEN. But who on earth is your Julia?

GADD. Ha! (*A cautious look towards* TELFER, *who is now up* L.C.) Mrs. Telfer *goes on* for it—a venerable stop-gap. Absurd, of course; but we daren't keep my Clifford from them any longer.

IMOGEN. You'll miss Rose Trelawny in business pretty badly, I expect, Gadd?

GADD (*with a shrug of the shoulders*). She was to have done Rosalind for my benefit. (*Producing play-bill, which* IMOGEN *takes and looks at.*) Miss Fitzhugh joins on Monday; I must pull *her* through it somehow. I would reconsider my bill, but they're waiting for my Orlando, waiting for it——

(*They continue their conversation in dumb-show.* COLPOYS *enters—an insignificant, wizen little fellow who is unable to forget that he is a low-comedian. He stands* L., *squinting hideously at* IMOGEN *and indulging in extravagant gestures of endearment.*)

COLPOYS (*failing to attract her attention, he kneels* L.C.). My love! my life!

IMOGEN (*nodding to him, indifferently, over the bill*). Good afternoon, Augustus.

COLPOYS (*ridiculously*). She speaks! she hears me! (*He rises. Finding* ABLETT *amused, he goes up* L. *of table, and taking up tablespoon, pretends to stab himself and sinks on chair, putting spoon back.*)

ABLETT (*holding his glove before his mouth, convulsed with laughter*). Ho, ho! oh, Mr. Colpoys! oh, reelly, sir! ho, dear!

GADD (*aside to* IMOGEN, *darkly*). Colpoys is not nearly as funny as he was last year. Everybody's saying so. We want a low-comedian badly.

(*He retires, deposits his hat on the wig-block, and joins* TELFER *and* TOM.)

COLPOYS (*rising—staggering to* IMOGEN *and throwing his arms about her neck*). Ah—h—h! after all these years!

IMOGEN (*pushing him away*). Do be careful of my things, Colpoys!

(COLPOYS *returns to chair* L. *of table and pretends to cry, and then wrings tears from handkerchief.*)

ABLETT (*going out, blind with mirth*). Ha, ha, ha! ho, ho!

(*He collides with* MRS. TELFER, *who is entering at this moment.* MRS. TELFER *is a tall, massive lady of middle age—a faded queen of tragedy.*)

(*As he disappears.*) I'm sure I beg your pardon, Mrs. Telfer, ma'am.

MRS. TELFER (*in a deep tone*). Violent fellow! (*Advancing to* IMOGEN *and kissing her solemnly.*) How is it with you, Jenny Parrott?

IMOGEN (R.C.). Thank you, Mrs. Telfer, as well as can be. And you?

MRS. TELFER (C., *waving away the inquiry*). I am obliged to you for this response to my invitation.

(COLPOYS *gets on chair, and makes grimaces, behind her back, to* IMOGEN.)

It struck me as fitting that at such a time you should return for a brief hour or two to the company of your old associates——

(COLPOYS, *behind* MRS. TELFER, *is still making grimaces at* IMOGEN.)

(*Becoming conscious of this.*) Eh—h—h? (*Turning to* COLPOYS *and surprising him.*) Oh—h—h!

(COLPOYS *gets off chair quickly.*)

Yes, Augustus Colpoys, you are extremely humorous *off*.

COLPOYS (*stung*). Miss Sylvester—Mrs. Telfer!

MRS. TELFER. *On* the stage, sir, you are enough to make a cat weep.

COLPOYS. Madam! from one artist to another! well, I——! 'Pon my soul! (*Retreating to up* L.C., *talking under his breath.*) Popular favourite! draw more money than all the—old guys——

MRS. TELFER (*following him*). What do you say, sir! Do you mutter!

(*They explain mutually up* L. AVONIA BUNN *enters—an untidy, tawdrily dressed young woman of about three-and-twenty, with the airs of a suburban soubrette. She wears a lace shawl and carries a pink parasol.*)

AVONIA (*embracing* IMOGEN R.C.). Dear old girl!

IMOGEN. Well, Avonia?

AVONIA. This is jolly, seeing you again. My eye, what a rigout! She'll be up directly. (*With a gulp.*) She's taking a last look-round at our room.

IMOGEN. You've been crying, 'Vonia.

AVONIA (C.). No, I haven't. (*Breaking down.*) If I have I can't help it. Rose and I have chummed together—all this season—and part of last—and—it's a hateful profession! The moment you make a friend——! (*Looking towards the door.*) There! isn't she a dream? I dressed her——

(*She moves away, up the stage* R., *as* ROSE TRELAWNY *and* ARTHUR GOWER *enter.* ROSE *is nineteen, wears washed muslin, and looks divine. She has much of the extravagance of gesture, over-emphasis in speech, and freedom of manner engendered by the theatre, but is graceful and charming nevertheless.* ARTHUR *is a handsome, boyish young man—" all eyes " for* ROSE.

As ROSE *and* ARTHUR *enter,* AVONIA *backs up* R., *looking admiringly at* ROSE, *then looks at table—calls* COLPOYS' *attention to it, and is going up when* GADD *offers to embrace her. She pushes him off, goes to piano, looks in mirror, and puts shawl and parasol on piano.*)

ROSE (*meeting* IMOGEN C.). Dear Imogen!

IMOGEN (*kissing her*). Rose dear!

(ARTHUR *gets* L.C.)

ROSE (C.). To think of your journeying from the West to see me make my exit from Brydon Crescent. But you're a good sort; you always were. Do sit down and tell me—oh——! Let me introduce Mr. Gower. Mr. Arthur Gower—Miss Imogen Parrott. *The* Miss Parrott, of the Olympic.

ARTHUR (*on* ROSE'S L., *reverentially*). I know. I've seen Miss Parrott as Jupiter, and as—I forget the name—in the new comedy ——

(IMOGEN R.C., *and* ROSE C., *sit, below the table.*)

ROSE. He forgets everything but the parts *I* play, and the pieces *I* play in—poor child! Don't you, Arthur?

ARTHUR (*standing by* ROSE, *looking down upon her*). Yes—no. Well, of course I do! How can I help it, Miss Parrott? Miss Parrott won't think the worse of me for that—will you, Miss Parrott?

(ROSE *takes off her gloves.*)

MRS. TELFER (*coming down* L.C.). I am going to remove my bonnet. Imogen Parrott——?

IMOGEN. Thank you, I'll keep my hat on, Mrs. Telfer—take care!

(MRS. TELFER, *in turning to go, encounters* ABLETT, *who is entering with two jugs of beer. Some of the beer is spilt.* Avonia, r. *of table, laughs.*)

Ablett. I beg your pardon, ma'am.

Mrs. Telfer (*examining her skirt*). Ruffian!

(*She departs.*)

Rose (*to* Arthur). Go and talk to the boys. I haven't seen Miss Parrott for ages.

(Arthur *goes down in semicircle to* l., *and then up* l., *and comes against* Ablett, *who comes down after putting jugs on sideboard up* l.)

Ablett. I beg your pardon, sir.

Arthur. I beg yours.

Ablett (*grasping* Arthur's *hand*). Excuse the freedom, sir, if freedom you regard it as——

Arthur. Eh——?

Ablett. You 'ave plucked the flower, sir; you 'ave stole our ch'icest blossom.

Arthur (*trying to get away*). Yes, yes, I know——

Ablett. Cherish it, Mr. Glover——!

Arthur. I will, I will. Thank you—— (*He goes up* l. *and puts his hat and stick down.*)

(Mrs. Mossop's *voice is heard calling* "Ablett!" Ablett *releases* Arthur *and goes out.* Arthur *joins* Colpoys *and* Tom, *up stage.* Colpoys *measures his height against* Arthur's.)

Rose (*to* Imogen). The carriage will be here in half an hour. (*She clutches* Imogen's *arm with her right hand, extending her left, theatrically.*) I've so much to say to you. Imogen, the brilliant hits you've made! How lucky you have been!

Imogen. *My* luck! What about *yours*?

(Avonia *joins group up* c.)

Rose (*leaning back in chair, right hand on table*). Yes, isn't this a wonderful stroke of fortune for me! Fate, Jenny! that's what it is—Fate! (*Extending her left hand to front.*) Fate ordains that I shall be a well-to-do fashionable lady, instead of a popular but toiling actress. Mother often used to stare into my face, when I was little, and whisper, "Rosie, I wonder what is to be your—fate." (*She raises her head and looks up to front.*) Poor mother! I hope she *sees.*

Imogen. Your Arthur seems nice.

Rose. Oh, he's a dear. Very young, of course—not much more than a year older than me—than I. But he'll grow manly in time, and have moustaches, and whiskers out to here, he says.

Imogen. How did you——?

ROSE. He saw me act Blanche in "The Pedlar of Marseilles," and fell in love.

IMOGEN. Do you prefer Blanche——?

ROSE. To Celestine? Oh, yes. You see, I got leave to introduce a song—(*looking towards* R.) where Blanche is waiting for Raphael on the bridge.

(GADD *comes down to the table to pick a flower from the dish, and puts it in his buttonhole.*)

(*Singing, dramatically but in low tones.*) "Ever of thee I'm fondly dreaming——"

IMOGEN. I know——

(*They sing together.*)

ROSE.
IMOGEN. } "Thy gentle voice my spirit can cheer."

ROSE. It was singing that song that sealed my destiny, Arthur declares. At any rate, the next thing was he began sending bouquets (*gesture of arm to* R.) and coming to the stage-door. (*Gesture of arm to* L.) Of course, I never spoke to him, never glanced at him. (*Hands clasped on lap.*) Poor mother brought me up in that way, not to speak to anybody, nor look.

IMOGEN. Quite right.

ROSE (*her head up*). I do hope she sees.

IMOGEN. And then——?

ROSE. Then Arthur managed to get acquainted with the Telfers, and Mrs. Telfer presented him to me. Mrs. Telfer has kept an eye on me all through. Not that it was necessary, brought up as I was—but she's a kind old soul.

IMOGEN. And now you're going to live with his people for a time, aren't you?

ROSE. Yes—on approval.

(AVONIA *gets* R. *of table.*)

IMOGEN. Ha, ha, ha! you don't mean that!

ROSE. Well, in a way—just to reassure them, as they put it. The Gowers have such odd ideas about theatres, and actors and actresses.

IMOGEN. Do you think you'll like the arrangement?

ROSE. It'll only be for a little while. I fancy they're prepared to take to me, especially Miss Trafalgar Gower——

IMOGEN. Trafalgar!

ROSE. Sir William's sister; she was born Trafalgar year, and christened after it——

(MRS. MOSSOP *and* ABLETT *enter, carrying trays on which are a pile of plates and various dishes of cold food—a joint, a chicken and tongue, a ham, a pigeon pie, etc. They proceed to set out the dishes on the table.* ROSE *and* IMOGEN *rise and go* R. ABLETT *drops a glove down* L.C. *as he enters.*)

AVONIA. Here comes the food! Oh, we are going to have a jolly time.

(*General chatter.* COLPOYS *takes the pigeon pie and, putting it on his head, trots round in front of table to* R. *of it.*)

Now, Gus, you'll drop it—don't be silly! Put it down!

(COLPOYS *puts it on the table, and* AVONIA *brings bread to* L. *on table.* ARTHUR *takes joints and vegetables from* MRS. MOSSOP *and places them* L. *on table.* ABLETT *goes up and, assisted by* TELFER *and others, places ham, tongue, vegetables, etc., up* C. *and* R. *on table.* MRS. MOSSOP *cuts bread.* ABLETT *pours out beer and then puts jug up* L.)

IMOGEN (R., *cheerfully*). Well, God bless you, my dear. I'm afraid *I* couldn't give up the stage though, not for all the Arthurs——

ROSE (L. *of* IMOGEN). Ah, your mother wasn't an actress.

IMOGEN. No.

ROSE. Mine was, and I remember her saying to me once, "Rose, if ever you have the chance, get out of it."

IMOGEN. The Profession?

ROSE. Yes. "Get out of it"; Mother said, "If ever a good man comes along, and offers to marry you and to take you off the stage, seize the chance—get out of it."

IMOGEN. Your mother was never popular, was she?

ROSE. Yes, indeed she was, most popular—till she grew oldish and lost her looks.

IMOGEN. Oh, *that's* what she meant then?

ROSE. Yes, that's what she meant.

(ABLETT *picks up his glove.*)

IMOGEN (*shivering*). Oh, lor', doesn't it make one feel depressed! (*Looks at table.*)

ROSE. Poor Mother! Well, I hope she sees.

MRS. MOSSOP (L.C.). Now, ladies and gentlemen, everything is prepared—

(*A general murmur of satisfaction.*)

—and I do trust to your pleasure and satisfaction.

TELFER (*up* C.). Ladies and gentlemen, I beg you to be seated.

(*There is a general movement.*)

Miss Trelawny will sit 'ere, on my right.

(AVONIA *runs up behind armchair to* L. *of it, and she and* GADD *move it for* ROSE *to sit in.*)

On my left, my friend Mr. Gower will sit.

(COLPOYS *moves chair for* ARTHUR.)

Next to Miss Trelawny—who will sit beside Miss Trelawny?

GADD. }
COLPOYS. } I will.

(COLPOYS *pushes* TELFER *out of his way, and runs to* R. *for seat.*)

AVONIA. No, do let me! (*She is pushed up stage by* COLPOYS.)

(GADD, COLPOYS, *and* AVONIA *gather round* ROSE *and wrangle for the vacant place;* IMOGEN *is down* R., TOM *up by mantel.*)

ROSE (*standing by her chair*). It must be a gentleman, 'Vonia.—Now, if you two boys quarrel——!

GADD. Please don't push me, Colpoys! } (*Both trying to sit*
COLPOYS. 'Pon my soul, Gadd——! } *down.*)

ROSE. I know how to settle it. Tom Wrench——!

TOM (*coming to her quickly*). Yes?

(COLPOYS *and* GADD *come down* R.C., *arguing.*)

IMOGEN (*seating herself below table* C., *after* ABLETT *has turned chair for her*). Mr. Gadd and Mr. Colpoys shall sit by me, one on each side.

(COLPOYS *takes chair* R.C., *next to* IMOGEN. GADD *comes to him and makes him move.* COLPOYS *then crosses and takes a chair* L.C., *next to* IMOGEN. AVONIA *sits next to* GADD, *but remembering the bread, she rises, goes above table to* L., *and hands bread round, chattering as she does so.* MRS. MOSSOP *sits on the* R. *of* COLPOYS. *Amid much chatter, the viands are carved by* MRS. MOSSOP, TELFER, *and* TOM. *Some plates of chicken, etc., are handed round by* ABLETT, *while others are passed about by those at the table. Then the chatter subsides.*)

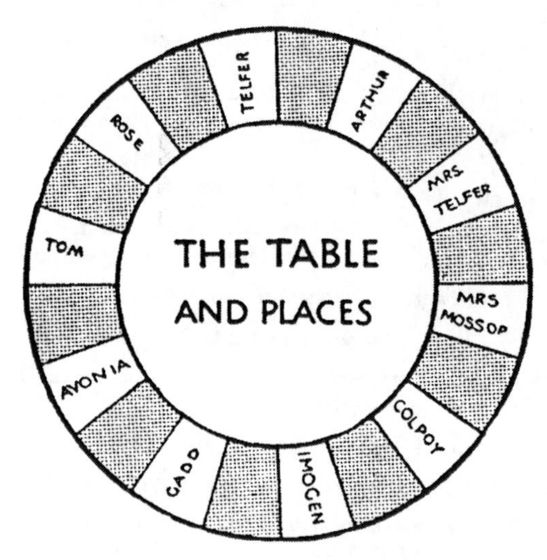

TELFER (*handing plate to* ARTHUR). Mr. Gower——

GADD (*during a pause in the hubbub, aside to* IMOGEN *and turning his chair to half face the audience*). Telfer takes the chair, you observe. Why *he*—more than myself, for instance ?

IMOGEN (*to* GADD). The Telfers have lent their room——

(AVONIA *sits after handing bread, and finding* GADD *has not been served she hands a plate to* TOM, *who holds it to* TELFER *for tongue and leg of chicken. He then returns it, and* AVONIA *puts it before* GADD.)

GADD. Their stuffy room ! That's no excuse. I repeat, Telfer has thrust himself into this position.

IMOGEN. He's the oldest man present.

GADD. True. And he begins to age in his acting too. His H's ! scarce as pearls !

IMOGEN (*nodding*). Yes, that's shocking. Now, at the Olympic, slip an H and you're damned for ever.

GADD. And he's losing all his teeth. To act with him, it makes the house seem half empty.

(AVONIA *calls his attention to plate.*)

(ABLETT *is now going about pouring out the ale. Occasionally he drops his glove, misses it, and recovers it. There is a buzz of conversation, which ceases as* TELFER *speaks.*)

TELFER (*to* IMOGEN). Miss Parrott, my dear, follow the counsel of one who has sat at many a "good man's feast"—have a little 'am.

IMOGEN. Thanks, Mr. Telfer. (*She rises and holds out plate over table.*)

(MRS. TELFER *returns.*)

MRS. TELFER. Sitting down to table in my absence !

(ROSE *rises nervously—the rest retaining whatever position they may be in—until* MRS. TELFER *is seated.* ARTHUR *rises and places chair for her to sit in.*)

(*To* TELFER.) How is this, James ?

TELFER. We are pressed for time, Violet, my love.

ROSE. Very sorry, Mrs. Telfer.

MRS. TELFER (*taking her place between* ARTHUR *and* MRS. MOSSOP —*gloomily*). A strange proceeding.

ROSE. Rehearsal was over so late. (*She sits and speaks—to* TELFER.) You didn't get to the last act till a quarter to one, did you ?

AVONIA (*taking off her hat and flinging it across the table to* COLPOYS). Gus ! catch ! Put it on the sofa, there's a dear boy.

(COLPOYS *perches the hat upon his head, and behaves in a ridiculous, mincing way.* ABLETT *is again convulsed with laughter. Some of the others are amused also, but more moderately.*)

(*Rising—fork in hand.*) Take that off, Gus! Mr. Colpoys, you just take my hat off! Put it down! You'll spoil the feathers. Gus!

(COLPOYS *rises, imitating the manners of a woman, and deposits the hat on the sofa.* AVONIA *keeps on talking until he is seated again.*)

ABLETT (*up the stage*). Ho, ho, ho! oh, don't, Mr. Colpoys! oh, don't, sir!

(COLPOYS *returns to the table, dancing.*)

GADD (*knife and fork in hand—aside to* IMOGEN). It makes me sick to watch Colpoys in private life. He'd stand on his head in the street, if he could get a ragged infant to laugh at him. (*He puts down knife and fork, takes up leg of fowl, and turns again half-round. Picking the leg of a fowl furiously.*) What I say is this. Why can't an actor, in private life, be simply a gentleman? (*Loudly and haughtily.*) More tongue here!

ABLETT (*hurrying to him*). Yessir, certainly, sir.

(COLPOYS *throws up pieces of bread, trying to catch them in his mouth as they fall. The others laugh.*)

(*Again discomposed by this antic on the part of* COLPOYS.) Oh, don't, Mr. Colpoys! (*Going to* TELFER *with* GADD'S *plate—speaking to* TELFER *while* TELFER *carves a slice of tongue.*) I shan't easily forget this afternoon, Mr. Telfer. (*Exhausted.*) This'll be something to tell Mrs. Ablett. Ho, ho! oh, dear, oh, dear!

(ABLETT *comes down* R., *averting his face from* COLPOYS, *and brings back* GADD'S *plate. By an unfortunate chance,* ABLETT'S *glove has found its way to the plate and is handed to* GADD *by* ABLETT.)

GADD (*picking up the glove in disgust*). Merciful powers! What's this!

ABLETT (R., *taking the glove*). I beg your pardon, sir—my error, entirely.

(*A firm rat-tat-tat at the front door is heard. There is a general exclamation. At the same moment* SARAH, *a diminutive servant, in a crinoline, appears in the doorway.*)

SARAH (*breathlessly*). The kerridge has just drove up!

ALL. The carriage! The carriage!

(IMOGEN *and* GADD *go to lower window.* COLPOYS *and* AVONIA *go to upper window.* MRS. MOSSOP *hurries away, pushing* SARAH *before her.*)

TELFER. Dear me, dear me! before a single speech has been made.

AVONIA (*at the window up the stage*). Rose, do look!

IMOGEN (*at the window down the stage*). Come here, Rose!

ROSE (*shaking her head*). Ha, ha! I'm in no hurry; I shall see it often enough. Well, the time has arrived.

(TOM *turns, facing audience, and resting elbow on back of chair, with his chin in his hand, thinking.*)

(*Laying down her knife and fork.*) Oh, I'm so sorry, now.

TOM (*brusquely*). Are you? I'm glad.

ROSE. Glad! That *is* hateful of you, Tom Wrench!

ARTHUR (*looking at his watch*). The carriage is certainly two or three minutes before its time, Mr. Telfer.

TELFER. Two or three——! The speeches, my dear sir, the speeches!

(MRS. MOSSOP *returns, panting; those at windows turn to listen.*)

MRS. MOSSOP. The footman, a nice-looking young man with hazel eyes, says the carriage and pair can wait for a little bit. (*By her chair.*) They must be back by three, to take their lady into the Park—— (*She sits.*)

TELFER (*rising*). Ahem! Resume your seats, I beg. Ladies and gentlemen——

AVONIA. Wait, wait! We're not ready!

(COLPOYS *sits in* GADD'S *chair, but is put out of it by* GADD. *He then goes to his own chair and sits.* IMOGEN *and* AVONIA *return to their places.* ABLETT *stands* L., *by the door.*)

TELFER (*producing a paper from his breast-pocket*). Ladies and gentlemen, I devoted some time this morning to the preparation of a list of toasts. I now 'old that list in my hand. (*Half-facing audience, as before.*) The first toast—— (*He pauses, to assume a pair of spectacles.*)

GADD (*aside to* IMOGEN). *He* arranges the toast-list! *He!*

IMOGEN (*to* GADD). Hush!

(GADD *turns to table and eats.*)

TELFER. The first toast that figures 'ere is, naturally, that of The Queen. (*Laying his hand on* ARTHUR'S *shoulder.*) With my young friend's chariot at the door, his horses pawing restlessly and fretfully upon the stones, I am prevented from enlarging upon the merits of this toast. Suffice it, both Mrs. Telfer and I have had the honour of acting before Her Majesty upon no less than two occasions.

(AVONIA, *with uplifted knife and fork, utters a cry of surprise.*)

GADD (*to* IMOGEN). Tsch, tsch, tsch! an old story!

TELFER. Ladies and gentlemen, I give you—(*to* COLPOYS)—the malt is with you, Mr. Colpoys.

COLPOYS (*handing the ale to* TELFER). Here you are, Telfer.

(ARTHUR *takes jug and fills* TELFER'S *glass.*)

TELFER. I give you The Queen, coupling with that toast the name of Miss Violet Sylvester—Mrs. Telfer. Miss Sylvester has so frequently impersonated the various queens of tragedy that I cannot but feel she is a fitting person to acknowledge our expression of loyalty. (*Raising his glass.*) The Queen! And Miss Violet Sylvester!

ALL. The Queen! The Queen! And Miss Violet Sylvester!

(*All rise, except* MRS. TELFER, *and drink the toast. After drinking,* MRS. MOSSOP *passes her tumbler to* ABLETT.)

ABLETT. The Queen! Miss Vi'lent Sylvester!

(*He drinks, wipes edge of glass with glove, and returns the glass to* MRS. MOSSOP. *The company being re-seated,* MRS. TELFER *rises. Her reception is a polite one.*)

MRS. TELFER (*heavily*). Ladies and gentlemen, I have played fourteen or fifteen queens in my time——

TELFER. Thirteen, my love, to be exact; I was calculating this morning.

MRS. TELFER. Very well, I have played thirteen of 'em. And, as parts, they are not worth a tinker's oath. I thank you for the favour with which you have received me.

(*She sits; the applause is heartier. During the demonstration,* SARAH *appears in the doorway, with a kitchen chair.*)

ABLETT (*to* SARAH). Wot's all this?

SARAH (*to* ABLETT). Is the speeches on?

ABLETT. H'on! Yes, and you be h'off!

(SARAH *places the chair against the open door*—ABLETT *trying to stop her*—*and sits, full of determination. At intervals* ABLETT *vainly represents to her the impropriety of her proceeding.* ABLETT *replenishes glasses* R. CALPOYS *replenishes glasses* L.)

TELFER (*again rising*). Ladies and gentlemen. Bumpers, I charge ye! The toast I 'ad next intended to propose was Our Immortal Bard, Shakespeare, and I had meant, myself, to 'ave offered a few remarks in response——

GADD (*to* IMOGEN, *bitterly*). Ha!

TELFER. But with our friend's horses champing their bits, I am compelled—nay, forced—to postpone this toast to a later period of the day, and to give you now what we may justly designate the toast of the afternoon. Ladies and gentlemen, we are about to lose, to part with, one of our companions.

(AVONIA *cries.*)

AVONIA (*with a sob*). I detested her at first.

COLPOYS. Order!

(*Altercation between* SARAH *and* ABLETT.)

IMOGEN. Be quiet, 'Vonia!

TELFER. Her late mother an actress, herself made familiar with the stage from childhood if not from infancy, Miss Rose Trelawny—for I will no longer conceal from you that it is to Miss Trelawny I refer——

(*Loud applause.*)

Miss Trelawny is the stuff of which great actresses are made.

ALL. Hear, hear!

ABLETT (*softly*). 'Ear, 'ear!

TELFER. So much for the actress. Now for the young lady—nay, the woman, the gyirl. Rose is a good girl——

(*Loud applause, to which* ABLETT *and* SARAH *contribute largely.* AVONIA *rises, and saying,* "Oh Rose, darling," *impulsively embraces* ROSE. IMOGEN *rises and brings her back to her seat, then returns to her own.*)

A good girl——

MRS. TELFER (*rising and clutching a knife*). Yes, and I should like to hear anybody, man or woman——!

TELFER. She is a good girl, and will be long remembered by us as much for her private virtues as for the commanding authority of her genius.

(*More applause, during which there is a sharp altercation between* ABLETT *and* SARAH.)

And now, what has happened to "the expectancy and Rose of the fair state"?

IMOGEN. Good, Telfer! good! (*She raps table with knife-handle.*)

GADD (*to* IMOGEN). Tsch, tsch! forced! forced!

TELFER. I will tell you—(*impressively*) a man has crossed her path.

ABLETT (*in a low voice*). Shame!

MRS. MOSSOP (*turning to him*). Mr. Ablett!

TELFER. A man—ah, but also a gentle-man.

(*Applause.*)

That gentleman, with the modesty of youth—for I may tell you at once that 'e is not an old man—comes to us and asks us to give him this gyirl to wife. And, friends, we have done so. Riches this youthful pair will possess—but what is gold? May they be rich in each other's society, in each other's love! May they—I can wish them no greater joy—be as happy in their married life—as Miss

Sylvester and I 'ave been in ours! (*Raising his glass.*) Miss Rose Trelawny—Mr. Arthur Gower!

(*The toast is drunk by the company, upstanding.*)

THE COMPANY (*heartily*). Rose! dear Rose! Miss Rose Trelawny—Rose dear! (*In polite manner.*) Mr. Arthur Gower! Mr. Gower!

(*Three cheers are called for by* COLPOYS, *and given. Those who have risen, then sit.* ABLETT *in waving his arms throws glove up; it is caught by* SARAH, *who puts it on.* ABLETT *misses it, looks for it, and finding it, snatches it from her angrily; she giggles.*)

TELFER. Miss Trelawny.
ROSE (*weeping*). No, no, Mr. Telfer.
MRS. TELFER (*to* TELFER, *softly*). Let her be for a minute, James.
TELFER. Mr. Gower.

(ARTHUR *rises and is well received.*)

ARTHUR. Ladies and gentlemen, I—I would I were endowed with Mr. Telfer's flow of—of—of splendid eloquence.
TELFER. No, no!
ARTHUR. But I am no orator, no speaker, and therefore cannot tell you how highly—how—how deeply I appreciate the—the compliment——
ABLETT. You deserve it, Mr. Glover!
ALL. Hush!
ARTHUR. All I can say is that I regard Miss Trelawny in the light of a—a solemn charge, and I—I trust that, if ever I have the pleasure of—of meeting any of you again, I shall be able to render a good—a—a—satisfactory——

(*A murmur of applause.* AVONIA *says,* "Oh! isn't that nice!")

—satisfactory——
TOM (*half-rising—in an audible whisper*). Account.
ARTHUR. Account of the way—of the way—in which I—in which——

(*Loud applause.*)

Before I bring these observations to a conclusion, let me assure you that it has been a great privilege to me to meet—to have been thrown with—a band of artists—whose talents—whose striking talents—whose talents——

(TOM *gets uncomfortable, and half rises.*)

TOM (*kindly, behind his hand*). Sit down.
ARTHUR (*helplessly*). Whose talents not only interest and instruct the—the more refined residents of this district, but whose talents——
IMOGEN (*aside to* COLPOYS). Get him to sit down.

ARTHUR. The fame of whose talents, I should say——

COLPOYS (*aside to* MRS. MOSSOP). He's to sit down. Tell Mother Telfer.

ARTHUR. The fame of whose talents has spread to—to regions——

MRS. MOSSOP (*pushing her chair back—aside to* MRS. TELFER). They say he's to sit down.

ARTHUR. To—to quarters of the town—to quarters——

MRS. TELFER (*to* ARTHUR). Sit down!

ARTHUR. Eh?

MRS. TELFER. You finished long ago. Sit down.

ARTHUR. Thank you. I'm exceedingly sorry. Great heavens, how wretchedly I've done it!

(*He sits, burying his head in his hands. More applause.*)

TELFER. Rose, my child.

(ROSE *starts to her feet. The rest rise with her, and cheer again, and wave handkerchiefs. She goes from one to the other, round the table, embracing and kissing and crying over them all excitedly.* ROSE *kisses—*

1*st*, TELFER, *who says,* "Blessings on you, my child!"
2*nd*, TOM.
3*rd*, AVONIA.
4*th*, GADD.
5*th*, IMOGEN.
6*th*, COLPOYS.
7*th*, SARAH.
8*th*, MRS. MOSSOP.
9*th*, MRS. TELFER.

All utter good wishes, which are kept up till she is on chair. After being kissed, AVONIA *tries to follow* ROSE, *and is pushed out of the way by* IMOGEN, *who is going to piano. She then sinks in her chair, leaning on back, facing audience.*

SARAH *is kissed, but upon* ABLETT *is bestowed only a handshake, to his evident dissatisfaction. After being kissed,* IMOGEN *runs to the piano and strikes up the air of "Ever of Thee." When* ROSE *gets back to the place she mounts her chair, with the aid of* TOM *and* TELFER, *and faces them with flashing eyes. They pull the flowers out of the vases and throw them at her.*)

ROSE. Mr. Telfer, Mrs. Telfer! My friends! Boys!

(IMOGEN *stops playing.*)

Ladies and gentlemen! No, don't stop, Jenny! Go on!

(IMOGEN *plays again.*)

(*Singing, her arms stretched out to them.*) "Ever of thee I'm fondly dreaming. Thy gentle voice——" You remember! The song I sang in "The Pedlar of Marseilles"—which made Arthur fall in love with me! Well, I know I shall dream of *you*——

(GADD *seizes her hand.*)

—of all of you, very often, as the song says. Don't believe, (*wiping away her tears*) oh, don't believe that, because I shall have married a swell, you and the old "Wells"—the dear old "Wells"!——

(*Cheers.*)

(*Her hand on* TELFER'S *shoulder.*) You and the old "Wells" will have become nothing to me! No, many and many a night you will see me in the house, looking down at you from the Circle—me and my husband——

ARTHUR. Yes, yes, certainly!

ROSE (*with open arms*). And if you send for me I'll come behind the curtain to you, and sit with you and talk of bygone times, these times that end to-day. (*Turns to* TELFER *and then to* TOM.) And shall I tell you the moments which will be the happiest to me in my life, however happy I may be with Arthur? Why, whenever I find that I am recognized by people, and pointed out—people in the pit of a theatre, in the street, no matter where; and when I can fancy they're saying to each other, (*pointing*), "Look! that was Miss Trelawny! You remember—Trelawny! Trelawny of the 'Wells!'"——

(*They cry* "Trelawny!" *and* "Trelawny of the 'Wells!'" *and again* "Trelawny!" *wildly. Then there is the sound of a sharp rat-tat at the front door.* IMOGEN *leaves the piano and looks out of the window.*)

IMOGEN (*to somebody below*). What is it?

A VOICE. Miss Trelawny, ma'am. We can't wait.

(ARTHUR *comes down* L. *and gives money to* ABLETT.)

ROSE (*weakly*). Oh, help me down——

(*They assist her, and gather round her finally, and as the* CURTAIN *falls,* SARAH, *in* C., *is being kissed by* ROSE.)

ACT II

The SCENE *represents a spacious drawing-room in a house in Cavendish Square. The walls are sombre in tone, the ceiling dingy, the hangings, though rich, are faded, and altogether the appearance of the room is solemn, formal, and depressing. Up* R. *is a single door, opening on to the stage. On the* R., *almost immediately below this door, occupying nearly the entire space of the wall between it and the proscenium, are folding-doors supposed to admit to a further drawing-room. These doors are in three folds ; the upper fold only is used, and that opens off the stage. The wall on the* L. *of the stage is mainly occupied by three sash-windows. These windows should be glazed, or filled with "gelatine" to imitate glass. The wall at the back of the stage is divided into three parts, or panels, by two pilasters standing* R.C. *and* L.C. *Between the side wall and the* R.C. *pilaster, at some distance from the ground, hangs a large oil painting—a portrait of Sir William Gower in his judicial wig and robes. Between the side wall and the* L.C. *pilaster hangs a companion picture—a portrait of Miss Gower. In the* C. *of the back wall there is a large mirror with a painted reflection of the fireplace, and the mirror above it, which would naturally occupy the fourth wall of the room. In the* R. *and* L. *corners of the room there are marble columns supporting classical busts. Against the* R. *wall, in the space between the upper door and the folding-doors, stands another marble column ; upon this column there is an oil lamp. Beneath each of the pictures there is a chair ; and beneath the mirror a couch. Placed against each of the two upper windows is a chair ; against the lower window there are two chairs and a card-table.* R.C., *about half-way up the stage, is a small circular table. On the* L. *of this table there is a chair, on its* R. *another chair ; and between these two chairs, below the table, is a footstool. On the table there are two or three books.* L.C., *about two-thirds of the distance up the stage, is another table. On the* R. *of this table there is a chair, on its* L., *running down the stage, a couch. Behind the table stands a three-fold screen. A lamp is upon the table, and some newspapers. Also 2 packs of cards and card counters in bag, and an alabaster ornament under glass shade on the table.*

The lamps are lighted, but the curtains are not drawn, and outside the windows it is twilight.

When the CURTAIN *rises,* SIR WILLIAM GOWER *is seated,* R. *of* L.C. *table, asleep. A newspaper is over his head, concealing his face.*

MISS TRAFALGAR GOWER *is sitting at the farther end of the couch* L., *also asleep and with a newspaper over her head. At the lower end of this couch sits* MRS. DE FŒNIX—CLARA—*a young lady of nineteen, with a "married" air. She is engaged upon some crochet work. On the other side of the stage, on the* L. *of* R.C. *table,* ROSE *is seated, wearing the look of a boredom which has reached the stony stage. On the couch up* L. ARTHUR *sits, gazing at his boots, his hands in his pockets. On the* R. *of this couch stands* CAPTAIN DE FŒNIX. *He is leaning against the wall, his mouth open, his head thrown back, and his eyes closed.* DE FŒNIX *is a young man of seven-and-twenty—an example of the heavily whiskered "swell" of the period. Everybody is in dinner-dress. After a moment or two,* ARTHUR *rises and tiptoes down to* ROSE. CLARA *raises a warning finger and says* "Hush!" *He nods to her, in assent.*

ARTHUR (*on* ROSE'S L.—*in a whisper*). Quiet, isn't it?

ROSE (*to him, in a whisper*). Quiet! Arthur——! (*Clutching his arm.*) Oh, this dreadful half-hour after dinner, every, *every* evening!

ARTHUR (*creeping across to* R., *looking cautiously at sleepers, and sitting on the* R. *of* R.C. *table*). Grandfather and Aunt Trafalgar must wake up soon. They're longer than usual to-night.

ROSE (*to him, across the table*). Your sister Clara, over there, (*she looks over her right shoulder, towards* CLARA) and Captain de Fœnix—when they were courting, did they have to go through this?

ARTHUR (*with a nod*). Yes.

ROSE. And now that they are married, they still endure it!

ARTHUR. Yes.

ROSE. And we, when *we* are married, Arthur, shall *we*——?

ARTHUR. Yes. I suppose so.

ROSE (*passing her hand across her brow*). Phe—ew!

(DE FŒNIX, *fast asleep, is now swaying, and in danger of toppling over.* CLARA *grasps the situation and rises.*)

CLARA (*in a guttural whisper*). Ah, Frederick! no, no, no!

ROSE / ARTHUR } (*turning in their chairs*). Eh—what—? ah—h—h—h!

(*As* CLARA *reaches her husband, he lurches forward into her arms.*)

DE FŒNIX (*his eyes bolting*). Oh! who——?

CLARA. Frederick dear, wake!

DE FŒNIX (*dazed*). How did this occur?

CLARA. You were tottering, and I caught you.

DE FŒNIX (*collecting his senses*). I wemember. I placed myself in an upwight position, dearwest, to prewent myself dozing.

CLARA (*sinking on to the couch up* C.). How you alarmed me!

(*Seeing that* ROSE *is laughing,* DE FŒNIX *comes down to her.*)

de Fœnix (*in a low voice*). Might have been a vevy serwious accident, Miss Trelawny.

Rose (*seating herself on the footstool*). Never mind. (*Pointing to the chair she has vacated.*) Sit down and talk.

(*He glances at the old people and shakes his head.*)

(*Piteously.*) Oh, do, do, do! do sit down, and let us all have a jolly whisper.

(*He sits.*)

Thank you, Captain Fred. Go on! tell me something—anything; something about the military——

de Fœnix (*again looking at the old people, then wagging his finger at* Rose). I know; you want to get me into a wow. (*Settling himself into his chair.*) Howwid girl!

Rose (*despairingly*). Oh—h—h!

(*There is a brief pause and then the sound of a street-organ, playing in the distance, is heard. The air is "Ever of Thee."*)

Hark! (*Excitedly.*) Hark!

Clara.
Arthur. } Hush!
de Fœnix.

Rose (*heedlessly*). The song I sang in "The Pedlar"—"The Pedlar of Marseilles!" The song that used to make you cry, Arthur——!

(*They attempt vainly to hush her down.*)

(*Dramatically, in hoarse whispers.*) And then Raphael enters—comes on to the bridge. The music continues, softly. "Raphael, why have you kept me waiting? Man, do you wish to break my heart—(*thumping her breast*) a woman's hear—r—rt, Raphael?"

(Sir William *and* Miss Gower *suddenly whip off their newspapers and sit erect.* Miss Gower *wakes first. She folds newspaper precisely and puts it on sofa;* Sir William *throws his behind chair.* Sir William *is a grim, bullet-headed old gentleman of about seventy;* Miss Gower *a spare, prim lady, of gentle manners, verging upon sixty. They stare at each other for a moment, silently.*)

Sir William. What a hideous riot, Trafalgar!

Miss Gower. Rose dear, I hope I have been mistaken—but through my sleep I fancied I could hear you shrieking at the top of your voice.

(Sir William *gets on to his feet; all rise, except* Rose, *who remains seated sullenly.* Sir William *goes* c.; Arthur, *with a look of horror on finding the old people awake, clasps his hands.*)

Sir William (*emphatically*). Trafalgar, it is becoming impossible for you and me to obtain repose. (*Turning his head sharply.*) Ha! is not that a street-organ? (*To* MISS GOWER.) An organ?

MISS GOWER. Undoubtedly. An organ in the Square, at this hour of the evening—singularly out of place!

SIR WILLIAM (*looking round*). Well, well, well, does no one stir?

ROSE (*under her breath*). Oh, don't stop it! (*She clasps her hands.*)

(CLARA *goes out quickly, up* R. *With a great show of activity,* ARTHUR *and* DE FŒNIX *hurry up the stage* R.C. *and, when there, do nothing.*)

SIR WILLIAM (*coming upon* ROSE *and peering down at her*). What are ye upon the floor for, my dear? (*He looks around.*) Have we no cheers? (*To* MISS GOWER—*producing his snuff-box.*) Do we lack cheers here, Trafalgar? (*Goes* C.)

MISS GOWER (*crossing to* ROSE). My dear Rose! (*Raising her.*) Come, come, come, this is quite out of place! Young ladies do not crouch and huddle upon the ground—do they, William?

SIR WILLIAM (*taking snuff*). A moment ago I should have hazarded the opinion that they do not. (*Chuckling unpleasantly.*) He, he, he! (*Goes over to* L.C.)

(CLARA *returns. The organ-music ceases abruptly.*)

CLARA (*coming to* SIR WILLIAM, L.C.). Charles was just running out to stop the organ when I reached the hall, Grand-pa.

SIR WILLIAM (*going up to her and looking her full in the face*). Ye'd surely no intention, Clara, of venturing, yourself, into the public street—the open Square——?

CLARA (C., *faintly*). I meant only to wave at the man from the door——

MISS GOWER (R.C.). Oh, Clara, that would hardly have been in place!

SIR WILLIAM (*raising his hands*). In mercy's name, Trafalgar, what *is* befalling my household?

MISS GOWER (*bursting into tears*). Oh, William——!

(ROSE *and* CLARA *exchange looks and creep away and join the others up the stage.* ROSE *goes up* R. *of table,* CLARA *up* R.C. *This group looks apprehensively at the* GOWERS. MISS GOWER *totters to* SIR WILLIAM *and drops her head upon his breast.*)

SIR WILLIAM (*down* L.C.). Tut, tut, tut, tut!

MISS GOWER (*aside to him, between her sobs*). I—I—I—I know what is in your mind.

SIR WILLIAM (*drawing a long breath*). Ah—h—h—h!

MISS GOWER. Oh, my dear brother, be patient!

SIR WILLIAM. Patient!

MISS GOWER. Forgive me; I should have said hopeful. Be hopeful that I shall yet succeed in ameliorating the disturbing conditions which are affecting us so cruelly.

Sir William. Ye never will, Trafalgar; *I've* tried.

Miss Gower. Oh, do not despond already! I feel sure there are good ingredients in Rose's character. (*Clinging to him.*) In time, William, we shall shape her to be a fitting wife for our rash and unfortunate Arthur——

(*He shakes his head.*)

In time, William, in time!

Sir William (*soothing her*). Well, well, well! (*He crosses to* R.C.) There, there, there! (*Turns to her.*) At least, my dear sister, I am perfectly aweer that I possess in you the woman above all others whose example should compel such a transformation.

Miss Gower (*throwing her arms about his neck*). Oh, brother, what a compliment——!

Sir William. Tut, tut, tut!

(*He throws her arms off, and she gets back a step to* R. *He turns and goes up* C. *The group at back suddenly turn and face up stage; he looks at them, then turns again to* Miss Gower.)

And now, before Charles sets the card-table, don't you think we had better—eh, Trafalgar?

Miss Gower (*coming to him*). Yes, yes—our disagreeable duty.

(*All heads turn.*)

Let us discharge it.

(Sir William *crosses to* R., *taking snuff.* Miss Gower *goes up* R.C. *and holds out her hand to* Rose, *who takes it. There is a look of horror from all, they stare anxiously at* Sir William.)

(*To* Rose.) Rose dear, be seated. (*She goes over table to chair* R. *of it—to everybody.*) The Vice-Chancellor has something to say to us. Let us all be seated.

(*There is consternation among the young people. All sit—*Sir William L. *of* R.C. *table,* Miss Gower *on his right hand, at the other side of the table;* Rose *in the chair* R. *of* L.C. *table;* Arthur *on the couch* L.; *and* Clara *and* de Fœnix *on the couch up* C. Sir William *puts snuff-box on table.*)

Sir William (*peering about him*). Are ye seated?

Everybody. Yes.

Sir William. What I desire to say is this. When Miss Trelawny took up her residence here, it was thought proper, in the peculiar circumstances of the case, that you, Arthur—(*pointing a finger at* Arthur) you——

Arthur. Yes, sir.

Sir William. That you should remove yourself to the establishment of your sister Clara and her husband in Holles Street, round the corner——

ARTHUR. Yes, sir.

CLARA. Yes, Grand-pa.

DE FŒNIX. Certainly, Sir William.

SIR WILLIAM. Taking your food in this house, and spending other certain hours here, under the surveillance of your great-aunt Trafalgar. (*He takes her hand across table.*)

MISS GOWER. Yes, William.

SIR WILLIAM. This was considered to be a decorous, and, towards Miss Trelawny, a highly respectful, course to pursue.

ARTHUR. Yes, sir.

MISS GOWER. Any other course would have been out of place.

SIR WILLIAM. And yet—(*again extending a finger at* ARTHUR) what is this that is reported to me? (*He turns his chair to him.*)

ARTHUR. I don't know, sir.

SIR WILLIAM. I hear that ye have on several occasions, at night, after having quitted this house with Captain and Mrs. de Fœnix, been seen on the other side of the way, your back against the railings, gazing up at Miss Trelawny's window; and that you have remained in that position for a considerable space of time. Is this true, sir?

(SIR WILLIAM *and* MISS GOWER *exchange looks.*)

ROSE (*boldly*). Yes, Sir William.

SIR WILLIAM. I venture to put a question to my grandson, Miss Trelawny.

ARTHUR. Yes, sir, it is quite true.

SIR WILLIAM. Then, sir, let me acqueent you that these are not the manners, nor the practices, of a gentleman.

ARTHUR. No, sir?

SIR WILLIAM. No, sir, they are the manners, and the practices, of a Troubadour.

MISS GOWER. A troubadour in Cavendish Square! Quite out of place!

ARTHUR. I—I'm very sorry, sir; I—I never looked at it in that light.

SIR WILLIAM (*snuffing*). Ah—h—h—h! ho! pi—i—i—sh!

ARTHUR. But at the same time, sir, I daresay—of course I don't speak from precise knowledge—but I daresay there were a good many—a good many——

SIR WILLIAM. Good many—what, sir?

ARTHUR. A good many very respectable troubadours, sir——

ROSE (*starting to her feet, heroically and defiantly*). And what I wish to say, Sir William, is this. I wish to avow (*her arms extended*), to declare before the world (*she turns up stage, her arms still extended*), that Arthur and I have had many lengthy interviews while he has been stationed against those railings over there; (*pointing* L.) I murmuring to him softly from my bedroom window, he responding in tremulous whispers——

(*During* ROSE'S *speech,* ARTHUR *looks at her with amazement, then buries his face in his hands, while* SIR WILLIAM *and* MISS GOWER *exchange looks*—SIR WILLIAM *struggles to his feet.*)

SIR WILLIAM. You—you tell me such things——!

(*All rise except* ARTHUR.)

MISS GOWER (*she gets to front of table and* SIR WILLIAM *gives her his right hand, but is looking steadily at* ARTHUR). The Square, in which we have resided for years——! Our neighbours——!

SIR WILLIAM (*shaking a trembling hand at* ARTHUR). The—the character of my house——!

ARTHUR (*rising, with a petulant stamp of his foot*). Again I am extremely sorry, sir—but these are the only confidential conversations Rose and I now enjoy.

SIR WILLIAM (*turning upon* CLARA *and* DE FŒNIX). And you, (*he goes up* C. *a little*) Captain de Fœnix—an officer and a gentleman! And you, Clara! This could scarcely have been without your cognizance, without, perhaps, your approval——!

(MISS GOWER, *going up* R., *agrees in dumb show.* CAPTAIN *and* MRS. DE FŒNIX *shrink away towards* L. CHARLES *enters, door up* R., *carrying two branch candlesticks with lighted candles.* CHARLES *is in plush and powder and wears luxuriant whiskers.*)

CHARLES (*up* R.C.). The cawd-table, Sir William?

MISS GOWER (*agitatedly—crossing to* SIR WILLIAM). Yes, yes, by all means, Charles; the card-table, as usual.

(CHARLES *carries the candlesticks to the table.*)

(*To* SIR WILLIAM.) A rubber will comfort you, soothe you——

(SIR WILLIAM *and* MISS GOWER *seat themselves upon the couch up* C., *she with her arm through his, affectionately.* CLARA *and* DE FŒNIX *get behind the screen; their scared faces are seen occasionally over the top of it.* CHARLES *brings the card-table from* L. *to* L.C., *opens it and arranges it, placing four chairs, which he collects from different parts of the room, round the table. Then he brings down the candles from table* L.C., *and also cards and a bag of counters, to card-table.* ROSE *crosses to* R.C., *followed by* ARTHUR. *They talk in rapid undertones.*)

ROSE. Infamous! Infamous!

ARTHUR (*on her* L.). Be calm, Rose dear, be calm!

ROSE. Tyrannical! diabolical! I cannot endure it.

(*She throws herself into the chair* R. *of* R.C. *table. He stands behind her, apprehensively, endeavouring to calm her.*)

ARTHUR (*over her shoulder*). They mean well, dearest——

ROSE (*hysterically*). Well! ha, ha, ha!

ARTHUR (*above table*). But they are rather old-fashioned people——

ROSE. Old-fashioned!—they belong to the time when men and women were put to the torture. I am being tortured—mentally tortured——

ARTHUR (*behind the* R.C. *table*). They have not many more years in this world——

ROSE. Nor I, at this rate, many more months. (*She turns to look up at* ARTHUR.) They are killing me—like Agnes in "*The Spectre of St. Ives.*" She expires, in the fourth act, as I shall die in Cavendish Square, painfully, of no recognized disorder——

(*The two appear above the screen.*)

ARTHUR. And anything we can do to make them happy——

ROSE. To make the Vice-Chancellor happy! I won't try! I will not! He's a fiend, a vampire——!

ARTHUR. Oh, hush!

ROSE (*snatching up* SIR WILLIAM'S *snuff-box which he has left upon the table*). His snuff-box! (*Rising and going to* R., *she opens box.*) I wish I could poison his snuff, as Lucrezia Borgia would have done. (*Turns sharply to* ARTHUR, *who is* R. *of table.*) *She* would have removed him within two hours of my arrival—I mean, her arrival. (*Opening the snuff-box and mimicking* SIR WILLIAM.) And here he sits and lectures me, and dictates to me! to Miss Trelawny! (*Long snort, and stamp of foot.*) "I venture to put a question to my grandson, Miss Trelawny!" Ha, ha! (*Taking a pinch of snuff thoughtlessly but vigorously.*) "Yah—h—h—h! pish!" (*Comes down a little towards table.*) "Have we no cheers? Do we lack cheers here, Trafalgar?" (*Suddenly.*) Oh——!

ARTHUR. What have you done?

ROSE (*in suspense, replacing the snuff-box* L. *of table*). The snuff——!

ARTHUR. Rose dear! (*He gives her his handkerchief.*)

ROSE (*putting her handkerchief to her nose, and rising*). Ah——!

(CHARLES, *having prepared the card-table, and arranged the candlesticks upon it, has withdrawn.* MISS GOWER *and* SIR WILLIAM *now rise.*)

MISS GOWER. The table is prepared, William. (*Coming down* C., *followed by* SIR WILLIAM.) Arthur, I assume you would prefer to sit and contemplate Rose——?

ARTHUR. Thank you, Aunt.

(ROSE *sneezes violently, and is led away, helplessly, by* ARTHUR *to up* R.C. SIR WILLIAM *looks surprised and annoyed.*)

MISS GOWER (*to* ROSE). Oh, my dear child! (*Looking round.*) Where are Frederick and Clara?

CLARA / DE FŒNIX } (*appearing from behind the screen, shamefacedly*). Here.

(*The intending players cut the pack, and seat themselves.* SIR WILLIAM *sits up the stage,* CAPTAIN DE FŒNIX *facing him,* MISS GOWER *on the* R. *of the table, and* CLARA *on the* L. CLARA *cuts.* CAPTAIN DE FŒNIX *deals.*)

ARTHUR (*while this is going on, to* ROSE). Are you in pain, dearest? Rose!

ROSE. Agony!

ARTHUR. Pinch your upper lip——

(*She sneezes twice, loudly, and sinks back upon the couch up* C.)

SIR WILLIAM (*rising—testily*). Sssh! sssh! sssh! This is to be whist, I hope.

MISS GOWER. Rose, Rose! young ladies do not sneeze quite so continuously.

(DE FŒNIX *is dealing.*)

SIR WILLIAM (*leaning over table—with gusto*). I will thank you, Captain de Fœnix, to exercise your intelligence this evening to its furthest limit.

DE FŒNIX. I'll twy, sir. (*He gets as far away in his chair from* SIR WILLIAM *as possible, with his feet behind the back of the chair.*)

SIR WILLIAM (*laughing unpleasantly*). He, he, he! Last night, sir——

CLARA. Poor Frederick had toothache last night, Grandpa.

SIR WILLIAM (*tartly*). Whist is whist, Clara, and toothache is toothache.

(CLARA, *frightened, slightly pushes her chair back.*)

We will endeavour to keep the two things distinct, if you please. He, he!

MISS GOWER. Your interruption was hardly in place, Clara dear—ah!

(*The deal is finished.*)

DE FŒNIX. Hey! what——?

MISS GOWER. A misdeal.

CLARA (*faintly*). Oh, Frederick!

SIR WILLIAM (*partly rising*). Captain de Fœnix!

DE FŒNIX. I—I'm fwightfully gwieved, sir—— (*Some business with chair.*)

(*The cards are re-dealt by* MISS GOWER. ROSE *now gives way to a violent paroxysm of sneezing.* SIR WILLIAM *rises and goes up* C.)

MISS GOWER. William——!

(*The players rise.*)

SIR WILLIAM (*angrily—to the players*). Is this whist, may I ask ?

(*They sit.*)

(*Standing.*) Miss Trelawny——

ROSE (*weakly*). I—I think I had better—what d'ye call it ?—withdraw for a few moments.

SIR WILLIAM (*sitting again*). Do so.

(ROSE *disappears up* R. ARTHUR *is leaving the room with her, but pauses and looks cautiously at the players before going.*)

MISS GOWER (*sharply*). Arthur! where are you going ?

ARTHUR (*returning promptly*). I beg your pardon, Aunt.

MISS GOWER. Really, Arthur——!

SIR WILLIAM (*rapping upon the table*). Tsch, tsch, tsch!

MISS GOWER. Forgive me, William.

(*They play.* SIR WILLIAM *leads. The others play quickly, and the trick is taken by* CLARA, *who leads the second card quickly; and this* MISS GOWER *trumps.*)

SIR WILLIAM (*intent upon his cards*). My snuff-box, Arthur; be so obleeging as to search for it.

ARTHUR (*brightly*). I'll bring it to you, sir. It is on the——

SIR WILLIAM. Keep your voice down, sir. We are playing—(*emphatically throwing down a card, as fourth player*) whist. Mine.

MISS GOWER (*picking up the trick*). No, William.

SIR WILLIAM (*glaring*). No!

MISS GOWER. I played a trump.

DE FŒNIX. Yes, sir, Aunt Trafalgar played a trump—the seven——

SIR WILLIAM. I will not trouble you, Captain de Fœnix, to echo Miss Gower's information.

DE FŒNIX. Vevy sowwy, sir.

MISS GOWER (*gently*). It *was* a *little* out of place, Frederick.

SIR WILLIAM. Sssh! whist.

(MISS GOWER *leads.* ARTHUR *is now on* SIR WILLIAM'S R., *with the snuff-box.*)

(*To* ARTHUR.) Eh ? what ? (*Taking the snuff-box.*) Oh, thank ye. Much obleeged, much obleeged.

(ARTHUR *walks away to* R.C. *and picks up a book.* SIR WILLIAM *turns in his chair, watching* ARTHUR.)

MISS GOWER. You to play, William. (*A pause.*) William, dear—— ?

(*She also turns, following the direction of his gaze. Laying down his cards, he leaves the card-table and goes over to* ARTHUR *slowly. Those at the card-table look on apprehensively.*)

Sir William (*in a queer voice*). Arthur.

Arthur (*shutting his book*). Excuse me, Grandfather.

Sir William. Ye—ye're a troublesome young man, Arthur.

Arthur. I—I don't mean to be one, sir.

Sir William. As your poor father was, before ye. And if you are fool enough to marry, and to beget children, doubtless your son will follow the same course. (*Taking snuff.*) Y—y—yes, but I shall be dead 'n' gone by that time, it's likely. Ah—h—h—h ! pi—i—i—sh ! I shall be sitting in the Court Above by that time——

(*From the adjoining room, down* R., *comes the sound of* Rose's *voice singing* "*Ever of Thee*" *to the piano. There is great consternation at the card-table.* Captain *and* Clara de Fœnix *rise quietly and get more* L. *They all rise.* Miss Gower *gets over to* R.C. *as* Sir William *crosses back to card-table.* Arthur *is moving towards the folding-doors.*)

(*Detaining him—quietly.*) No, no, let her go on, I beg. Let her continue. (*Returning to the card-table, with deadly calmness.*) We will suspend our game while this young lady performs her operas.

Miss Gower (*taking his arm*). William——!

Sir William (*in the same tone*). I fear this is no longer a comfortable home for ye, Trafalgar ; no longer the home for a gentlewoman. I apprehend that in these days my house approaches somewhat closely to a Pandemonium. (*Suddenly taking up the cards, in a fury, and flinging them across the room over his head.*) And this is whist—whist——!

(Clara *and* de Fœnix *stand together* L.C. Arthur *pushes open the upper part of the folding-doors.*)

Arthur. Rose ! stop ! Rose !

(*The song ceases and* Rose *appears.*)

Rose (*at the folding-doors*). Did anyone call ?

Arthur (*above* R.C. *table*). You have upset my grandfather.

Miss Gower (C.). Miss Trelawny, how—how dare you do anything so—so out of place ?

Rose (*advancing to below* R.C. *table and pointing off* R.). There's a piano in there, Miss Gower.

Miss Gower. You are acquainted with the rule of this household —no music when the Vice-Chancellor is within doors.

Rose (*below table* R.). But there are so many rules. One of them is that you may not sneeze.

Miss Gower (C.). Ha ! you must never answer——

Rose. No, that's another rule.

Miss Gower. Oh, for shame !

Arthur (*up by chair* R.C.). You see, Aunt, Rose is young, and—and—you make no allowance for her, give her no chance——

MISS GOWER. Great heaven! what is this you are charging me with?

ARTHUR. I don't think the "rules" of this house are fair to Rose! Oh, I must say it—they are horribly unfair!

MISS GOWER (*clinging to* SIR WILLIAM). Brother!

SIR WILLIAM. Trafalgar! (*Putting her aside to* L.C. *and advancing to* ARTHUR.) Oh, indeed, sir! And so you deliberately accuse your great-aunt of acting towards ye and Miss Trelawny *malâ fide*——

ARTHUR. Grandfather, what I intended to——

SIR WILLIAM. I will afford ye the opportunity of explaining what ye intended to convey, downstairs, (*pointing down*) at once, in the library. (*He points again.*)

(*A general shudder.*)

Obleege me by following me, sir. (*To* CLARA *and* DE FŒNIX.) Captain de Fœnix——

(*He comes down a little*—CAPTAIN DE FŒNIX *starts violently on being addressed.*)

I see no prospect of any further social relaxation this evening. You and Clara will do me the favour of attending in the hall, in readiness to take this young man back to Holles Street. (*Going up and giving his arm to* MISS GOWER.) My dear sister—— (*To* ARTHUR.) Now, sir.

(SIR WILLIAM *and* MISS GOWER *go out up* R. ARTHUR *comes to* ROSE *and kisses her.*)

ARTHUR. Good night, dearest. Oh, good night! Oh, Rose——!

SIR WILLIAM (*outside the door*). Mr. Arthur Gower!

ARTHUR. I am coming, sir——

(*He goes out quickly up* R.)

DE FŒNIX (*approaching* ROSE *and taking her hand sympathetically*). Haw——! I—weally—haw!——

ROSE. Yes, I know what you would say. Thank you, Captain Fred.

(CAPTAIN DE FŒNIX *goes up near door* R.)

CLARA (*coming across quickly and embracing* ROSE). Never mind! We will continue to let Arthur out at night as usual. I am a married woman! (*joining* DE FŒNIX) and a married woman will turn, if you tread upon her often enough——!

(DE FŒNIX *and* CLARA *depart.*)

ROSE (*pacing the room up* C., *then down and round card-table to up* L.C., *shaking her hands in the air desperately*). Oh—h—h! ah—h—h!

(*The upper part of the folding-doors opens, and* CHARLES *appears.*)

CHARLES (*mysteriously*). Miss Rose——

ROSE. What——?

CHARLES (*advancing to up* R.C.). I see Sir William h'and the rest descend the stairs. I 'ave been awaitin' the chawnce of 'andin' you this, Miss Rose.

(*He produces a dirty scrap of paper, wet and limp, with writing upon it, and gives it to her.*)

ROSE (*handling it daintily*). Oh, it's damp!——

CHARLES. Yes, miss; a little gentle shower 'ave been takin' place h'outside—'eat spots, cook says.

ROSE (*coming down* L.C., *reading*). Ah! from some of my friends.

CHARLES (*behind his hand*). Perfesshunnal, Miss Rose? (*He gets near table* R.C.)

ROSE (*intent upon the note*). Yes—yes——

CHARLES. I was reprimandin' the organ, miss, when I observed them lollin' (*he jerks his thumb towards* L.) against the square railin's examinin' h'our premises, and they wentured for to beckon me. An egstremely h'affable party, miss. (*Hiding his face.*) Ho! one of them caused me to laff!

ROSE (*excitedly*). They want to speak to me—(*referring to the note*) to impart something to me, of an important nature. Oh, Charles, I know not what to do. (*She goes up* C. *and walks to and fro.*)

CHARLES (*right hand on table, right leg across his* L.—*languishingly*). Whatever friends may loll against them railin's h'opposite, Miss Rose, you 'ave one true friend in this 'ouse—(*touches his breast*) Chawles Gibbons——

ROSE (*nodding*). Thank you, Charles. Mr. Briggs, the butler, is sleeping out to-night, isn't he? (*She comes down* C.)

CHARLES. Yes, miss, he 'ave leave to sleep at his sister's. I 'appen to know he 'ave gone to Cremorne.

ROSE. Then, when Sir William and Miss Gower have retired, do you think you could let me go forth; and wait at the front door while I run across and grant my friends a hurried interview?

CHARLES. Suttingly, miss.

ROSE. If it reached the ears of Sir William, or Miss Gower, you would lose your place, Charles!

CHARLES (*haughtily*). I'm aweer, miss; but Sir William was egstremely rood to me dooring dinner, over that mis'ap to the ontray——

(*A bell rings violently.*)

S'william!

(*He goes out up* R. *The rain is heard pattering against the window-panes.* ROSE *goes from one window to another, looking out. It is now almost black outside the windows.*)

ROSE (*discovering her friends*). Ah ! yes, yes ! ah—h—h—h !

(*She snatches an antimacassar from a chair and, jumping on to the couch* L., *waves it frantically to those outside.*)

The dears ! the darlings ! the faithful creatures——! (*Listening.*) Oh——!

(*She descends, in a hurry, and flings the antimacassar under the couch, as* MISS GOWER *enters, up* R. *At the same moment there is a vivid flash of lightning.*)

MISS GOWER (*startled*). Oh, how dreadful ! (C., *to* ROSE, *frigidly.*) The Vice-Chancellor has *felt* the few words he has addressed to Arthur, and has retired for the night.

(*There is a roll of thunder.* ROSE *crosses to* R.C., *alarmed.*)

(*Clinging to a chair,* R.C.) Mercy on us ! Go to bed, child, directly. We will all go to our beds, hoping to awake to-morrow in a meeker and more submissive spirit. (*Kissing* ROSE *upon the brow.*) Good night.

(*Another flash of lightning.*)

Oh——! Don't omit to say your prayers, Rose—and in a simple manner. I always fear that, from your (*coming to* L.C.) peculiar training, you may declaim them. That is so out of place—(*clinging to chair*) oh——!

(*Another roll of thunder.* ROSE *goes up the stage,* R. *of table, meeting* CHARLES, *who enters carrying a lantern. They exchange significant glances, and she disappears.*)

CHARLES (*coming to* MISS GOWER). I am now at liberty to accompany you round the 'ouse, ma'am——

(*A flash of lightning.*)

MISS GOWER. Ah——! (*Her hand to her heart.*) Thank you, Charles—but to-night I must ask you to see that everything is secure, alone. This storm—so very seasonable ; but, from girlhood, I could never——

(*A roll of thunder.*)

Oh, good night.

(*She flutters away, up* R. *The rain beats still more violently upon the window-panes.* CHARLES *puts lantern down* C.)

CHARLES (*glancing at the window*). Ph—e—e—w ! Great 'evans !

(*He is dropping the curtains at the window down* L., *when* ROSE *appears at the folding-doors.*)

ROSE (*in a whisper*). Charles !

Charles. Miss?

Rose (*coming into the room, distractedly*). Miss Gower has gone to bed.

Charles. Yes, miss—oh——!

(*A flash of lightning*—Charles *recoils.*)

Rose. Oh! my friends! my poor friends!

Charles (*in front of card-table*). *H'and* Mr. Briggs at Cremorne! (*Meeting her*, c.) Reelly, I should 'ardly advise you to wenture h'out, miss——

Rose. Out! No! Oh, but get them in!

Charles. *In*, Miss Rose! indoors!

Rose. Under cover——

(*A roll of thunder.*)

(*Sitting* R.C.) Oh! (*Wringing her hands.*) They are my friends! Is it a rule that I am never to see a friend, that I mayn't even give a friend shelter in a violent storm? (*Rising—to* Charles.) Are you the only one up?

Charles. I b'lieve so, miss. Any'ow the wimming-servants is quite h'under my control.

Rose. Then tell my friends to be deathly quiet, and to creep—to tiptoe——

(*The rain strikes the window again. She picks up the lantern, which* Charles *has deposited upon the floor, and gives it to him.*)

Make haste! I'll draw the curtains——

(*He hurries out, up* R. *She goes from window to window, dropping the curtains, talking to herself excitedly as she does so.*)

My friends! my own friends! ha! (*She comes from upper window above screen and down to card-table.*) I'm not to sneeze in this house! nor to sing! or breathe, next! wretches! oh, my! wretches! (*Blowing out the candles and removing the candlesticks to the table* L.C.—*singing, under her breath, wildly.*) "Ever of thee I'm fondly dreaming——" (*Mimicking* Sir William *again.*) "What are ye upon the floor for, my dear? Have we no cheers? Do we lack cheers here, Trafalgar——?"

(Charles *returns, up* R.)

Charles (*to those who follow him*). Hush! (*Up* R.C., *to* Rose.) I discovered 'em clustered in the doorway——

(*There is a final peal of thunder as* Avonia, Gadd, Colpoys, *and* Tom Wrench *enter, somewhat diffidently. They are apparently soaked to their skins, and are altogether in a deplorable condition.* Avonia *alone has an umbrella, which she allows to drip upon the carpet, but her dress and petticoats are bedraggled, her finery limp, her hair lank and loose.*)

ROSE (*down* L.C.). 'Vonia!

AVONIA (*coming to her, and embracing her fervently*). Oh, ducky, ducky, ducky! Oh, but what a storm!

ROSE. Hush! How wet you are!

(*A pause—to allow* AVONIA *to walk up* C., *showing her petticoat.*)

(*Shaking hands with* GADD, C.) Ferdinand—(*crossing to* COLPOYS, *down* R.C., *and shaking hands with him*) Augustus—(*shaking hands with* TOM, R.) Tom, Wrench——

AVONIA (*to* CHARLES, *up the stage*). Be so kind as to put my umbrella on the landing, will you? Oh, thank you very much, I'm sure.

(CHARLES *withdraws with the umbrella.* GADD *and* COLPOYS *shake the rain from their hats on to the carpet and furniture.*)

TOM (*quietly, to* ROSE—*on her* R.). It's a shame to come down on you in this way. But they would do it, and I thought I'd better stick to 'em.

GADD (*down* L., *who is a little flushed and unsteady*). Ha! (*Scraping boots on chair-rail.*) I shall remember this accursed evening.

AVONIA (*coming down on* ROSE'S L.). Oh, Ferdy——!

ROSE. Hush! you must be quiet. Everybody has gone to bed, and I—I'm not sure I'm allowed to receive visitors——

AVONIA. Oh!

GADD. Then we are intruders?

ROSE. I mean, such late visitors.

(COLPOYS *is now at the back of the stage. He has taken off his coat, and is shaking it vigorously.*)

AVONIA. Stop it, Augustus! Ain't I wet enough? (*To* ROSE.) Yes, it is latish, but I so wanted to inform you—here—— (*She beckons to* GADD.) Allow me to introduce—my husband. (*She takes his arms.*)

ROSE. Oh, no!

AVONIA (*laughing merrily*). Yes! ha, ha, ha!

ROSE. Sssh, sssh, sssh!

AVONIA. I forgot. (*To* GADD.) Oh, darling Ferdy, you're positively soaked! (*To* ROSE.) Do let him take his coat off, like Gussy——

GADD (*jealously*). 'Vonia, not so much of the Gussy!

AVONIA. There you are, flying out again! As if Mr. Colpoys wasn't an old friend!

GADD. Old friend or no old friend——

ROSE (*diplomatically*). Certainly, take your coat off, Ferdinand.

(GADD *joins* COLPOYS *up* C.; *they spread out their coats upon the couch up* C.)

(*Feeling* TOM'S *coat-sleeve.*) And you?

TOM (*after glancing at the others—quietly*). No, thank you.

AVONIA (*sitting front of card-table*). Yes, dearie, Ferdy and I were married yesterday.

ROSE (*sitting* L. *of* R.C. *table*). Yesterday!

AVONIA. Yesterday morning. We're on our honeymoon now. You know, the "Wells" shut a fortnight after you left us, and neither Ferdy nor me could fix anything, just for the present, elsewhere; and as we hadn't put-by during the season—you know it never struck us to put-by during the season—we thought we'd get married.

(GADD *comes down and sits on card-table with his foot on chair* R. *of it; he looks down on* AVONIA *lovingly.*)

ROSE (*nodding*). Oh, yes.

AVONIA. You see, a man and his wife can live almost on what keeps one, rent *and* ceterer; and so, being deeply attached, as I tell you, we went off to church and did the deed. Oh, it will be such a save. (*Looking up at* GADD *coyly.*) Oh, Ferdy——!

GADD (*laying his hand upon her head, dreamily*). Yes, child, I confess I love you——

COLPOYS (*behind* ROSE, *imitating* GADD). Child, I confess I adore you.

TOM (*taking* COLPOYS *by the arm and swinging him away from* ROSE). Enough of that, Colpoys!

COLPOYS. What!

ROSE (*rising*). Hush!

TOM (*under his breath*). If you've never learnt how to behave——

COLPOYS. Don't you teach behaviour, sir, to a gentleman who plays a superior line of business to yourself! (*Muttering.*) 'Pon my soul! rum start——!

(*He turns and goes up* L.C. TOM *follows to up* C., *then looks round the room at the decorations and architecture.*)

AVONIA (*going to* ROSE, *down* R.C.). Of course I ought to have written to you, dear, properly, but you remember the weeks it takes me to write a letter——

(GADD *sits in the chair his foot has been on.* AVONIA *returns and seats herself upon his knee.*)

And so I said to Ferdy, over tea, "Ferdy, let's spend a bit of our honeymoon in doing the West End thoroughly, and going and seeing where Rose Trelawny lives." And we thought it only nice and polite to invite Tom Wrench and Gussy——

GADD. 'Vonia, much less of the Gussy!

AVONIA (*kissing* GADD). Jealous boy! (*Beaming.*) Oh, and we *have* done the West End thoroughly.

(COLPOYS *comes to back of card-table and sits, collects the cards and begins to build a house.*)

There, I've never done the West End so thoroughly in my life! And when we got outside your house I couldn't resist—— (*Her hand on* Gadd's *shirt-sleeve.*) Oh, gracious! I'm sure you'll catch your death, my darling——!

Rose. I think I can get him some wine. (*To* Gadd.) Will you take some wine, Ferdinand?

(Gadd *rises, nearly upsetting* Avonia.)

Avonia. Ferdy!

Gadd. I thank you. (*With a wave of the hand.*) Anything, anything——

Avonia (*to* Rose). Anything that goes with stout, dear.

Rose (*at the door up* r., *turning to them*). 'Vonia—boys—be very still.

(Avonia *goes up* c. *a little.*)

Avonia. Trust *us*!

(*She takes her hat off and goes down to* r. *corner, wiping it with a handkerchief;* Gadd *goes* l.)

(Rose *tiptoes out.* Colpoys *is now at the card-table, cutting a pack of cards which remains there.*)

Colpoys (*to* Gadd). Gadd, I'll see you for pennies.

Gadd (*loftily*). Done, sir, with you!

(*They seat themselves at the table,* Colpoys *up the stage,* Gadd *on the* l. *of the table, and cut for coppers.* Tom *is walking about, surveying the room.*)

Avonia (*down* r.c.). Well, Thomas, what do you think of it?

Tom (c.). *This* is the kind of chamber I want for the second act of my comedy——

Avonia. Oh, lor', your head's continually running on your comedy. Half this blessed evening——

Tom (*coming down* c. *a little*). I tell you, I won't have doors stuck here, there, and everywhere; no, nor windows in all sorts of impossible places! (*He goes up* l.c., *looking about him.*)

Avonia. Oh, really! Well, when you do get your play accepted, mind you see that Mr. Manager gives you exactly what you ask for—won't you?

Tom (*turning quickly and coming down* c.). You needn't be satirical, if you *are* wet. Yes, I will! (*Pointing to the* l.) Windows on the one side, (*pointing to the* r.) doors on the other—just where they should be, architecturally. And locks on the doors, *real locks*, to work; and handles—to turn! (*Rubbing his hands together gleefully.*) Ha, ha! you wait! wait——! (*Goes up* l.c.)

(Rose *re-enters up* r., *a plate of biscuits in her hand, followed by* Charles, *who carries a decanter of sherry and some wine-glasses.*)

ROSE (*above the* R.C. *table*). Here, Charles——

(CHARLES *places the decanter and the glasses on the table.*)

GADD (*whose luck has been against him, throwing himself, sulkily, on to the couch* L.). Bah! I'll risk no further stake.

COLPOYS (*rising and going to* C.). Just because you lose sevenpence in coppers you go on like this!

(CHARLES, *turning from the table, faces* COLPOYS.)

(*Tearing his hair, and glaring at* CHARLES *wildly.*) Ah—h—h, I am ruined! I have lost my all! my children are beggars——! (*He throws himself on the card-table and vibrates one of his legs violently.*)

CHARLES. Ho, ho, ho! he, he, he!

ROSE. Hush, hush!

(CHARLES *goes out, laughing, quietly.*)

(*To everybody.*) Sherry.

GADD (*rising*). Sherry?

(COLPOYS *crosses* R. GADD *rises and goes down* L., *in front of card-table, and thence across to table* R.C. *They help themselves to sherry and biscuits.*)

ROSE (*to* TOM, *up* C.). Tom, won't you——?

TOM (*watching* GADD *anxiously*). No, thank you. The fact is, we—we have already partaken of refreshments, once or twice during the evening——

(COLPOYS *and* AVONIA, *each carrying a glass of wine and munching a biscuit, cross, down the stage, to the couch* L.C., *where they sit.* AVONIA *sits above* COLPOYS *on the couch.*)

GADD (R.C., *pouring out sherry—singing*). "And let me the canakin clink, clink—and let me the canakin——"

ROSE (*coming to him*). Be quiet, Gadd!

COLPOYS (*raising his glass*). The Bride!

(TOM *gets quietly across at back to* R.)

ROSE (*turning, kissing her hand to* AVONIA). Yes, yes——

(GADD *hands* ROSE *his glass; she puts her lips to it.*)

The Bride! (*She returns the glass to* GADD.)

GADD (*sitting* L. *of* R.C. *table*). My Bride!

(TOM, *from behind the table, unperceived, takes the decanter and hides it under the table; then sits* R. GADD, *missing the decanter, sits and contents himself with the biscuits.*)

AVONIA (*on sofa* L.C.). Well, Rose, my darling, we've been talking about nothing but ourselves. How are you getting along here?

ROSE (C.). Getting along? Oh, I—I don't fancy I'm getting along very well, thank you.

COLPOYS }
AVONIA } (*on sofa* L.). Not——!

GADD (*sitting* R.C., *his mouth full of biscuit*). Not——!

ROSE (*sitting above the card-table*). No, boys; no, 'Vonia. The truth is, it isn't as nice as you'd think it. I suppose the Profession had its drawbacks—mother used to say so—but (*raising her arms*) one could fly. Yes, in Brydon Crescent one was a dirty little London sparrow perhaps; but here, in this grand square——! Oh, it's the story of the caged bird, over again.

AVONIA. A love-bird, though.

ROSE. Poor Arthur? Yes, he's a dear. (*Rising.*) But the Gowers—the old Gowers! the Gowers! the Gowers!

AVONIA. }
COLPOYS. } The Gowers! What does she mean by "the Gowers"?

(ROSE *paces the room, beating her hands together. In her excitement, she ceases to whisper, and gradually becomes loud and voluble. The others, following her lead, chatter noisily—excepting* TOM, *who sits, thoughtfully, looking before him.*)

ROSE. The ancient Gowers! the venerable Gowers!

AVONIA. You mean, the grandfather——?

ROSE. And the aunt—the great-aunt—the great bore of a great-aunt! The very mention of 'em makes something go "tap, tap, tap, tap" at the top of my head.

AVONIA. Oh, I *am* sorry to hear this. Well, upon my word——!

ROSE (C.). Would you believe it? 'Vonia—boys—you'll never believe it! I mayn't walk out with Arthur alone, nor see him here alone. I mayn't sing; no, nor sneeze even——

AVONIA (*shrilly*). Not sing or sneeze!

COLPOYS (*indignantly*). Not sneeze!

ROSE. No, nor sit on the floor—the *floor*! (*She walks to and fro up* C., *then sits on sofa up* C.)

AVONIA. Why, when we shared rooms together, you were always on the floor!

GADD (*producing a pipe, and knocking out the ashes on the heel of his boot*). In heaven's name, what kind of house can this be!

AVONIA. I wouldn't stand it, would you, Ferdinand? (*She puts glass on table above sofa.*)

GADD (*loading his pipe*). Gad, no!

AVONIA (*to* COLPOYS). Would you, Gus dear?

GADD (*glaring at them—under his breath*). Here! not so much of the Gus dear——

AVONIA (*to* COLPOYS). Would you?

COLPOYS. No, I'm blessed if I would, my darling.

GADD (*his pipe in his mouth*). Mr. Colpoys! less of the darling!

AVONIA (*rising*). Rose, don't you put up with it! (*Striking *the top of the card-table vigorously.*) I say, don't you stand it! (*Embracing* ROSE.) You're an independent girl, dear; they came to you, these people, not you to them, remember.

(COLPOYS *rises and puts his glass on table above sofa.*)

ROSE (*sitting on the couch up* C.). Oh, what can I do? I can't do anything.

AVONIA. Can't you! (*Coming to* GADD.) Ferdinand, advise her. You tell her how to——

GADD (*who has risen*). Miss Bunn—Mrs. Gadd, you have been all over Mr. Colpoys (*he points over her shoulder at* COLPOYS) this evening, ever since we——

AVONIA (*angrily, pushing him back into his chair*). Oh, don't be a silly!

GADD. Madam!

AVONIA (*returning above card-table to* COLPOYS). Gus, Ferdinand's foolish. Come and talk to Rose, and advise her, there's a dear boy——

(GADD *drops pipe.*)

(COLPOYS *rises; she takes his arm, to lead him to* ROSE. *At that moment* GADD *advances to* COLPOYS *and slaps his face violently.*)

COLPOYS. Hey——!

GADD. Miserable viper!

(*The two men close.* TOM *runs to separate them.* ROSE *rises with a cry of terror. There is a struggle and general uproar. The struggle is at first up* C.*—then down to* R.C.*, where* TOM *pulls* GADD *away to* R.*, while* COLPOYS *gets away to down* L. *Then* GADD *breaks away, and he and* COLPOYS *meet* C.*, and the struggle is renewed, and the card-table is overturned, with a crash, and* AVONIA, *down* R.C., *utters a long and piercing shriek. Then the house-bells are heard ringing violently.*)

ROSE. Oh——!

(*The combatants part; all look scared.*)

(*At the door, listening.*) They are moving—coming! Turn out the—— (*She shuts the door and goes to table.*)

(*She turns out the light at the table* L.C. *The stage is in half-light as* SIR WILLIAM *enters up* R.*, cautiously, closely followed by* MISS GOWER. *They are both in dressing-gowns and slippers;* SIR WILLIAM *carries a thick stick and his bedroom candle.* ROSE *is standing by the chair* R. *of* L.C. *table;* GADD, AVONIA, COLPOYS, *and* TOM *are together, down* L.)

SIR WILLIAM (R.C.). Miss Trelawny——!

MISS GOWER. Rose——! (*Running behind the screen.*) Men! (*Her head appears above screen.*)

Sir William (r.c.). Who are these people ?

Rose (*advancing a step or two*). Some friends of mine, who used to be at the "Wells," have called upon me, to inquire how I am getting on.

(Arthur *enters, up* r., *quickly.*)

Arthur (*up* r.c., *looking round*). Oh ! Rose——!

Sir William (*turning upon him*). Ah—h—h—h ! How come you here ?

Arthur. I was outside the house. Charles let me in, knowing something was wrong.

Sir William (*peering into his face*). Troubadouring—— ?

Arthur. Troubadouring ; yes, sir. (*To* Rose.) Rose, what is this ?

Sir William (*fiercely*). No, sir, this is my affair. (*Placing his candlestick on the* r.c. *table.*) Stand aside ! (*Raising his stick furiously.*) Stand aside !

(Arthur *comes down to* r.)

Miss Gower (*over the screen*). William——

Sir William. Hey ?

Miss Gower. Your ankles——

Sir William (*adjusting his dressing-gown*). I beg your pardon. (*To* Arthur.) Yes, I can answer your question. (*Pointing his stick, first at* Rose, *then at the group down* l.) Some friends of that young woman's, connected with—the play-house, have favoured us with a visit, for the purpose of ascertaining how she is—getting on. (*Touching* Gadd's *pipe, which is lying at his feet, with the end of his stick.*) A filthy tobacco-pipe. To whom does it belong ? (*Shrilly.*) Whose is it ?

(Arthur *is about to pick it up, but is stopped by* Sir William, *who puts his stick in the way.* Rose *picks it up and passes it to* Gadd, *bravely.*)

Rose. It belongs to one of my friends.

Sir William (*taking* Gadd's *empty wine-glass from the* r.c. *table, and holding it to his nose*). Phu, yes ! In brief, a drunken debauch. (*To the group.*) So ye see, gentlemen—(*to* Avonia) and you, madam ; (*to* Arthur) and you, sir ; you see, all of ye, (*sinking into chair,* r.c., *coughing from exhaustion*) exactly how Miss Trelawny is getting on.

Miss Gower (*over the screen*). William——

Sir William. What is it ?

Miss Gower. Your ankles——

Sir William (*leaping to his feet, in a frenzy*). Bah !

Miss Gower. Oh, they seem so out of place !

Sir William (*flourishing his stick—to the group down* l.). Begone ! A set of gairish, dissolute gipsies ! Begone !

(Gadd, Avonia, Colpoys, *and* Wrench *gather up* c., *the men hastily putting on their coats, etc.*)

Avonia (l.c.). Where's my umbrella?

Gadd. A hand with my coat here!

Colpoys (r.c.). 'Pon my soul! London artists——!

Avonia. We don't want to remain where we're not heartily welcome, I can assure everybody.

Sir William (*crossing to down* l.c.). Open windows! Let in the air!

Avonia (*coming to* l. *of* Rose, *who is standing* c., *above the wreck of the card-table*). Good-bye, my dear——

Rose. No, no, 'Vonia. Oh, don't leave me behind you!

(Gadd *gets over near door.*)

Arthur. Rose——!

Rose. Oh, I'm very sorry, Arthur. (*To* Sir William.) Indeed I am very sorry, Sir William. But you are right—gipsies—gipsies! (*To* Arthur.) Yes, Arthur, if you were a gipsy, as I am——

(*She goes up* c., *putting her arm round* Avonia*;* Colpoys, *on her* r., *takes her other hand.*)

—as these friends o' mine are, we might be happy together. (*She comes down* c.) But I've seen enough of your life, my dear boy, to know that I'm no wife for you. I should only be wretched, and would make you wretched; and the end, when it arrived, as it very soon would, would be much as it is to-night——!

Arthur (*distractedly*). You'll let me see you, talk to you, to-morrow, Rose?

(Tom *works quietly to down* r.)

Rose. No, never!

Sir William (*sharply*). You mean that?

Rose (*going over a little* l.c.—*facing him*). Oh, don't be afraid. I give you my word.

Sir William (*gripping her hand*). Thank ye. Thank ye.

Tom (*down* r., *behind* Arthur—*aside to him, quickly*). Mr. Gower, come and see *me* to-morrow—— (*He moves away to the door.*)

Rose (*turning to* Avonia, Gadd, *and* Colpoys, *who are together up* c.). I'm ready——

(Sir William *gets over more to* l.c.)

Miss Gower (*coming from behind the screen to the back of the couch,* l.). Not to-night, child, not to-night! Where will you go?

Avonia (*holding* Rose). To her old quarters in Brydon Crescent. Send her things after her, if you please.

Miss Gower. And then——?

Rose. Then back to the "Wells" again, Miss Gower!—back to the "Wells"——!

(*The* Curtain *falls.*)

ACT III

The SCENE *represents an apartment on the second floor of* MRS. MOSSOP'S *house. The room is of a humbler character than that shown in Act I; but, though shabby, it should be neat, and any suggestion of squalor should be avoided. On the* R., *a little more than half-way up the stage, is a door, outside which is supposed to be the landing. This door opens on to the stage, down the stage. In the wall at the back, between* R.C. *and* C., *is another door, presumably admitting to a further chamber; this door opens off the stage. Down* L. *there is a fireplace, with a fire burning, and over the mantelpiece a mirror. From the* C. *of the wall up the stage to the* C. *of the wall on the* L. *runs a stout cord supporting a pair of cur[illegible]ns of some common and faded material. At the opening of the act these curtains are shown drawn aside, disclosing, in the* L. *corner, a small bedstead with a tidily made bed. At the foot of the bedstead stands a large theatrical dress-basket filled with stage clothes, and containing the special objects revealed in the course of the act. By the head of the bed, against the* L. *wall, is a chair. On the wall, above this chair, are some pegs upon which hang a skirt or two and other articles of attire. Up* R., *against the back wall, there is a chest of drawers, the top of which is used as a washstand. In front of this is a small screen. On the wall, between the washstand and the door at the back, there are some more pegs with things hanging upon them. Above the door* R., *against the wall, there is a chair; and below the door* R., *against the wall, a sofa with its head down the stage. On the wall above the sofa there is a hanging bookcase and a few books. Under sofa, some old boots and two blue bonnet-boxes.* L.C., *about one third of the distance up the stage, there is a small circular table with a somewhat shabby cover upon it. On the table there are an inkstand, a blotting-book, envelopes and paper; also a duster and dusting-brush appertaining to* MRS. MOSSOP. *On the* R. *of this table is a chair; above the table, another chair; and on the* L. *of the table, turned to the fire, an armchair.*

The walls are papered, the doors painted stone-colour. An old felt carpet is on the floor. The light is that of morning.

(MRS. MOSSOP, *now dressed in a workaday gown, has just finished making the bed. There is a knock at the* C. *door.*)

AVONIA (*from the adjoining room*). Rose!

MRS. MOSSOP (*giving a final touch to the quilt*). Eh?

AVONIA. Is Miss Trelawny in her room?

MRS. MOSSOP (*going to the* C. *door*). No, Mrs. Gadd; she's at rehearsal.

AVONIA. Oh——

MRS. MOSSOP *draws the curtains, hiding the bed from view.* AVONIA *enters, door* R., *in a morning wrapper which has seen its best days. She carries a pair of curling-tongs, and her hair is evidently in process of being dressed in ringlets.*)

Of course she is; (*she shuts the door*) I forgot. There's a call for "The Pedlar of Marseilles." Thank Gawd, *I'm* not in it.

(*She comes* C.—*singing.*)

"I'm a great guerilla chief, I'm a robber and a thief——

(MRS. MOSSOP *laughs.*)

I can either kill a foe or prig a pocket-handkerchief——"

MRS. MOSSOP (*dusting the ornaments on the mantelpiece*). Bless your heart, you're very gay this morning!

AVONIA (L.C.). It's the pantomime. I'm always stark mad as the pantomime approaches. I don't grudge letting the rest of the company have their fling at other times—but with the panto comes *my* turn. (*Throwing herself full length upon the sofa gleefully.*) Ha, ha, ha! the turn of Avonia Bunn! (*Curling hair—with a change of tone.*) I hope Miss Trelawny won't take a walk up to Highbury, or anywhere, after rehearsal. I want to borrow her gilt belt. My dress has arrived.

MRS. MOSSOP (*much interested*). No! has it? (*She goes* C.)

AVONIA. Yes, Mrs. Burroughs is coming down from the theatre at twelve-thirty to see me in it.

(MRS. MOSSOP *goes up* R. *and draws the screen in front of the chest of drawers.*)

(*Singing.*) "Any kind of villainy cometh natural to me,
So it endeth with a combat and a one, two, three——!"[1]

MRS. MOSSOP (C., *surveying the room*). Well, that's as cheerful as I can make things look, poor dear!

AVONIA (*leaning on her elbow and taking a look round, seriously.*) It's pretty bright—if it wasn't for the idea of Rose Trelawny having to economize!

MRS. MOSSOP. Ah—h!

AVONIA (*rising and crossing to* L. *fiercely*). That's what I can't swallow. (*Sticking her irons in the fire angrily.*) One room! and on the second floor! (*Turning to* MRS. MOSSOP.) Of course, Gadd and me are one-room people too—(*glancing at the* C. *door*) and on the same floor; but then Gadd is so popular *out* of the theatre,

[1] These snatches of song are from "The Miller and His Men," a burlesque mealy-drama, by Francis Talfourd and Henry J. Byron, produced at the Strand Theatre, April 9th, 1860.

MRS. Mossop—he's obliged to spend such a load of money at the "Clown"—— (*She takes irons from fire.*)

MRS. MOSSOP (*who has been dusting the bookcase, coming to the table*). Mrs. Gadd, dearie, I'm sure I'm not in the least inquisitive; no one could accuse me of it—but I should like to know just one thing.

AVONIA (*testing her irons upon a sheet of paper which she takes from the table*). What's that? (*She turns to looking-glass* L.)

MRS. MOSSOP. Why *have* they been and cut down Miss Trelawny's salary at the "Wells"?

AVONIA (*hesitatingly*). H'm, everybody's chattering about it; you could get to hear easily enough—— (*She curls her hair in the glass.*)

MRS. MOSSOP. Oh, I daresay.

AVONIA. So I don't mind. Poor Rose! They tell her she can't act now, Mrs. Mossop.

MRS. MOSSOP. Can't act!

AVONIA (*turning to* MRS. MOSSOP). No, dear old girl, she's lost it; it's gone from her—the trick of it——

(TOM *enters, door* R., *carrying a table-cover of a bright pattern.*)

TOM (*coming upon* MRS. MOSSOP, *disconcerted*). Oh——!

MRS. MOSSOP. My first-floor table-cover!

TOM (*getting above table* L.C.). Y—y—yes.

(AVONIA *takes writing materials off the table and puts them in chair* L. *of it; then* TOM *takes off the old cover and throws it to* MRS. MOSSOP, *he puts on the new cover, and replaces the writing materials.*)

I thought, as the Telfers have departed, and as their late sitting-room is at present vacant, that Miss Trelawny might enjoy the benefit—hey?

MRS. MOSSOP. Well, I never——!

(*She goes out, door* R.)

AVONIA (*curling her hair, at the mirror over the mantelpiece*). I say, Tom, I wonder if I've done wrong——

TOM (*above table*). It all depends upon whether you've had the chance.

AVONIA. I've told Mrs. Mossop the reason they've reduced Rose's salary.

TOM. You needn't.

AVONIA (*turning to* TOM). She had only to ask any other member of the company——

TOM. To have found one who could have kept silent.

AVONIA (*remorsefully*). Oh, I could burn myself! (*She puts tongs in fire.*)

TOM. Besides, it isn't true.

AVONIA. What——?

TOM. That Rose Trelawny is no longer up to her work.

AVONIA (*sadly*). Oh, Tom! (*Takes tongs out.*)

TOM (*walking about*). It isn't the fact, I say!

AVONIA. Isn't it the fact that ever since Rose returned from Cavendish Square—— ?

TOM (*turning to* AVONIA). She has been reserved, subdued, lady-like——

AVONIA (*leaning over table—shrilly*). She was always lady-like!

TOM. I'm aware of that!

AVONIA. Well, then, what do you mean by—— ?

TOM (*in a rage, turning away*). Oh——! (*Goes* C.)

AVONIA (*heating her irons again*). The idea!

TOM (*cooling down*). She was always a lady-like *actress*, on the stage and off it, but now she has developed into a—(*at a loss*) into a——

AVONIA (*scornfully*). Ha! (*Curling her hair.*)

TOM. Into a lady-like human being. These fools at the "Wells"! (*He goes down to* R.C.) Can't act, can't she! No, she can no longer *spout*, she can no longer *ladle*, the vapid trash, the —the—the turgid rodomontade——

AVONIA (*front of table—doubtfully*). You'd better be careful of your language, Wrench.

TOM (C., *with a twinkle in his eye—mopping his brow*). You're a married woman, 'Vonia——

AVONIA (*holding her irons to her cheek, modestly*). I know, but still——

TOM (*coming* L.C.). Yes, deep down in the well of that girl's nature there has been lying a little, bright, clear pool of genuine refinement, girlish simplicity. And now the bucket has been lowered by love; experience has turned the handle; and up comes the crystal to the top, pure and sparkling. Why, her broken engagement to poor young Gower has really been the making of her! It has transformed her! (*Going* R.C. *thoughtfully.*) Can't act, can't she! (*Drawing a long breath.*) How she would play Dora in my comedy!

AVONIA. Ho, that comedy! (*Puts irons in fire.*)

TOM. How she would murmur those love-scenes!

AVONIA. Murder——!

TOM (*testily*). Murmur. (*Partly to himself.*) Do you know, 'Vonia, I had Rose in my mind when I imagined Dora—— ? (*He comes* C.)

AVONIA (*taking irons out*). Ha, ha! you astonish me.

TOM (*by chair* L.C., R. *of table*). And Arthur Gower when I wrote the character of Gerald, Dora's lover. (*In a low voice.*) Gerald and Dora—Rose and Arthur— (*he sits* L.C.) Gerald and Dora—— (*Turning to her—suddenly.*) 'Vonia——!

AVONIA (*singeing her hair*). Ah——! Oh, lor'! What now?

TOM. I wish you could keep a secret.

AVONIA. Why, can't I?

TOM. Haven't you just been gossiping with Mother Mossop?

AVONIA (*behind table, breathlessly, her eyes bolting*). A secret, Tom?

TOM (*nodding*). I should like to share it with you, because—you are fond of her too——

AVONIA (*on his* R.). Ah——!

TOM. And because the possession of it is worrying me. But there, I can't trust you.

AVONIA. Mr. Wrench!

TOM (*turning towards her*). No, you're a warm-hearted woman, 'Vonia, but you're a sieve.

AVONIA (*going down upon her knees beside him—very earnestly*). I swear! By all my hopes, Tom Wrench, of hitting 'em as Prince Charming in the coming pantomime, I swear I will not divulge, leave alone tell a living soul, any secret you may entrust to me, or let me know of, concerning Rose Trelawny of the "Wells." (*Facing audience.*) Amen!

TOM (*in her ear*). 'Vonia, *I know where Arthur Gower is.*

AVONIA (*turning to him—still on her knees*). *Is!* Isn't he still in London?

TOM (*producing a letter mysteriously*). No. When Rose stuck to her refusal to see him—listen—mind, not a word——!

AVONIA (*as before*). By all my hopes——!

TOM (*checking her*). All right, all right! (*Reading.*) "Theatre Royal, Bristol. Friday——"

AVONIA (*sitting on her heels*). Theatre Royal, Br——!

TOM. Be quiet! (*Reading—leaning towards her.*) "My dear Mr. Wrench. A whole week and not a line from you to tell me how Miss Trelawny is. When you are silent I am sleepless at night and a haggard wretch during the day. Young Mr. Kirby, our Walking Gentleman, has been unwell, and the management has given me temporarily some of his business to play——"

AVONIA (*on her knees*). Arthur Gower——!

TOM. Will you? (*Reading.*) "Last night I was allowed to appear as Careless in 'The School for Scandal.' Miss Mason, the Lady Teazle, complimented me, but the men said I lacked vigour" —the old cry!—"and so this morning I am greatly depressed." (*He half turns away, and leans his elbow on the table; she comes a little nearer to look over the letter.*) "But I will still persevere, as long as you can assure me that no presuming fellow is paying attention to Miss Trelawny. Oh, how badly she treated me!——"

AVONIA (*following the reading of the letter*). "How badly she treated me——!"

TOM. "I will never forgive her—only love her——"

AVONIA. "Only love her——"

TOM. "Only love her, and hope I may some day become a great actor, and, like herself, a gipsy. Yours very gratefully, Arthur Gordon."

AVONIA. In the Profession! (*She sinks back on her heels.*)

TOM. Bolted from Cavendish Square—went down to Bristol——

AVONIA. How did he manage it all?

(TOM *taps his breast proudly.*)

(*On her knees.*) But isn't Rose to be told? Why shouldn't she be told?

TOM. She has hurt the boy, stung him to the quick, and he's proud.

AVONIA. But she loves him now that she believes he has forgotten her. She only half-loved him before. She loves him!

TOM (*turning his face to* L.). Serve her right.

AVONIA. Oh, Tom, is she never to know?

TOM (*folding the letter carefully*). Some day, when he begins to make strides.

AVONIA. Strides! He's nothing but General Utility at present?

TOM (*putting the letter in his pocket*). No.

AVONIA. And how long have you been that?

TOM. Ten years.

AVONIA (*with a little screech*). Ah—h—h! She ought to be told!

TOM (*seizing her wrist*). Woman, you won't——!

AVONIA (*raising her disengaged hand*). By all my hopes of hitting 'em——!

TOM. All right, I believe you—— (*Listening.*) Sssh!

(*They rise and separate, he moving to the fire, she to the* R., *as* ROSE *enters at the door* R. ROSE *is now a grave, dignified, somewhat dreamy young woman and carries a reticule.*)

ROSE (*looking from* TOM *to* AVONIA). Ah——?

TOM.
AVONIA. } Good morning.

ROSE (*kissing* AVONIA). Visitors!

AVONIA. My fire's so black; (*showing her irons*) I thought you wouldn't mind——

ROSE (*going to* L.C., *removing her gloves*). Of course not. (*Puts reticule on table and gloves in it. Seeing the table-cover.*) Oh——!

TOM (*by fire—promptly*). Mrs. Mossop asked me to bring that upstairs. It was in the Telfers' room, you know, and she fancied——

ROSE. How good of her! Thanks, Tom. (*Taking off her hat and mantle.*) Poor Mr. and Mrs. Telfer! They still wander mournfully about the "Wells"; they can get nothing to do.

(*Carrying her hat and mantle and reticule, she disappears through the curtains.*)

TOM (*to* AVONIA, *in a whisper, across the room*). The Telfers——!

AVONIA. Eh?

TOM. She's been giving 'em money.

AVONIA (*nodding*). Yes.

TOM. Damn! (*Leans on mantelpiece.*)

ROSE (*reappearing*). What are you saying about me? (*Coming* C.)

AVONIA. I was wondering whether you'd lend me that belt you bought for Ophelia; to wear during the first two or three weeks of the pantomime——

ROSE (C., *kissing* AVONIA). Certainly, 'Vonia, to wear throughout——

AVONIA (*embracing her*). No, it's too good; I'd rather fake one for the rest of the time. (*Looking into her face.*) What's the matter?

ROSE. I will make you a present of the belt, 'Vonia, if you will accept it. I bought it when I came back to the "Wells," thinking everything would go on as before. But—it's of no use; they tell me I cannot act effectively any longer——

TOM (*indignantly*). Effectively——!

ROSE. First, as you know, they reduce my salary——

TOM
AVONIA } (*with clenched hands*). Yes!

ROSE. And now, this morning—(*pause—sitting* R. *of table; she looks at each of them in turn*) you can guess——

AVONIA (*hoarsely*). Got your notice?

ROSE. Yes.

TOM.
AVONIA. } Oh—h—h—h!

ROSE (*after a little pause*). Poor mother! I hope she doesn't see. (*She buries her face in her hands.*)

(*Overwhelmed,* AVONIA *and* TOM *sit and exchange looks, she above the table, he on the* L.)

I was running through Blanche, my old part in "The Pedlar of Marseilles," when Mr. Burroughs spoke to me.

(*The other two watch her earnestly.*)

It is true I was doing it tamely, but—it is such nonsense.

TOM. Hear, hear!

ROSE. And then, that poor little song I used to sing on the bridge——

AVONIA (*leaning towards* R. *and singing, softly*). "Ever of thee I'm fondly dreaming——"

TOM
AVONIA } (*singing*). "Thy gentle voice my spirit can cheer."

ROSE (*nods*). I told Mr. Burroughs I should cut it out. (*Thoughtfully.*) So ridiculously inappropriate!

TOM. And that—did it?

ROSE (*smiling at him*). That did it.

AVONIA (*kneeling beside her, on her* R., *and embracing her tearfully*).

My ducky! Oh, but there are other theatres besides the "Wells"
——

ROSE. For me?—only where the same trash is acted.

AVONIA (*with a sob*). But a few months ago you l—l—liked your work.

ROSE. Yes, (*dreamily*) and then I went to Cavendish Square, engaged to Arthur——

(TOM *rises and leans upon the mantelpiece, looking into the fire.*)

(*Reflectively.*) How badly I behaved in Cavendish Square! How unlike a young lady! What if the old folks *were* overbearing and tyrannical, Arthur could be gentle with them. "They have not many more years in this world," he said—dear boy!—"and anything we can do to make them happy——" (*She turns to* AVONIA.) And what *did* I do? *There* was a chance for me—to be patient, and womanly; and I proved to them that I was nothing but—an actress.

AVONIA (*rising, hurt but still tearful, and going* R.C.). It doesn't follow, because one is a——

ROSE (*facing* AVONIA). Yes, 'Vonia, it does! We are only dolls, partly human, with mechanical limbs that *will* fall into stagey postures, and heads stuffed with sayings out of rubbishy plays. (*She rises and goes to* AVONIA, C.) It isn't *the* world we live in, merely *a* world—such a queer little one! I was less than a month in Cavendish Square, and very few people came there; but they were *real* people—*real!*

(TOM *gets quietly, front of table, to* L.C.)

For a month I lost the smell of gas and oranges, and the hurry and noise, and the dirt and the slang, and the clownish joking, at the "Wells." I didn't realize at the time the change that was going on in me; I didn't realize it till I came back. And then, by degrees, I discovered what had happened——

(TOM *is now near her, on her* L. *She takes his hand and drops her head upon* AVONIA'S *shoulder.*)

(*Wearily.*) Oh, Tom! Oh, 'Vonia——!

(*From the next room comes the sound of the throwing about of heavy objects, and of* GADD'S *voice uttering loud imprecations.*)

(*Alarmed.*) Oh——!

(*Another sound outside.*)

AVONIA (*listening attentively*). Sounds like Ferdy.

(*She goes to the* C. *door.* ROSE *moves away to the fireplace,* TOM *to the* R. *Another sound.*)

(*At the keyhole.*) Ferdy! ain't you well, darling?

GADD (*on the other side of the door*). Avonia!

AVONIA. I'm in Miss Trelawny's room.

GADD. Ah——?

AVONIA (*to* ROSE *and* TOM). Now, what's put Ferdy out?

(GADD *enters door* R., *with a wild look.*)

(*Meeting him,* C.) Ferdinand!

TOM. Anything wrong, Gadd?

GADD (*looks at* TOM, *then crosses to* L.C.). Wrong! Wrong! (*Sitting* R. *of table.*) What d'ye think?

AVONIA (*on his* R.). Tell us!

GADD. I have been asked to appear in the pantomime.

AVONIA (*shocked*). Oh, Ferdy!—you!

GADD. I, a serious actor, if ever there was one; a poetic actor——!

AVONIA. What part, Ferdy?

GADD. The insult, the bitter insult! the gross indignity!

AVONIA. What part, Ferdy?

GADD. I who have not been seen in pantomime for years, not since I shook the dust of the T. R. Stockton from my feet.

AVONIA. Ferdy, what part?

GADD. I simply looked at Burroughs, when he preferred his request, and swept from the theatre.

AVONIA. What part, Ferdy?

GADD (*looking towards* ROSE). A part, too, which is seen for a moment at the opening of the pantomime, and not again till its close.

AVONIA. Ferdy.

GADD. Eh?

AVONIA. What part?

GADD. A character called the Demon of Discontent.

(ROSE *turns away to the fireplace;* TOM *curls himself up on the sofa and is seen to shake with laughter.*)

AVONIA (*walking about indignantly*). Oh! (*Returning to* GADD.) Oh, it's a rotten part! Rose dear, (*up* C.) I assure you, as artist to artist, that part is absolutely rotten. (*Returns to* GADD.) You won't play it, darling?

GADD (*rising*). Play it! I would see the "Wells" in ashes first.

AVONIA. We shall lose our engagements, Ferdy. I know Burroughs; we shall be out, both of us.

GADD. Of course we shall. D'ye think I have not counted the cost?

AVONIA (*putting her hand in his*). I don't mind, dear—for the sake of your position—(*struck by a sudden thought*) oh——!

GADD. What——?

AVONIA. There now—we haven't put-by!

(*There is a knock at the door* R.)

ROSE. Who is that?

COLPOYS (*outside the door*, R.). Is Gadd here, Miss Trelawny?

ROSE. Yes.

COLPOYS. I want to see him.

GADD. Wrench, I'll trouble you.

(TOM *rises quickly and comes to* C. *in mock humility to receive instructions.*)

Ask Mr. Colpoys whether he approaches me as a friend, an acquaintance, or in his capacity of stage-manager at the "Wells"—the tool of Burroughs.

(TOM *bows in stage manner, then goes* R. *and opens the door slightly.* GADD *and* AVONIA *join* ROSE *at the fireplace.*)

TOM (*at the door, solemnly*). Colpoys, are you here as Gadd's bosom friend, or as a mere tool of Burroughs?

(*An inaudible colloquy follows between* TOM *and* COLPOYS. *During the colloquy* AVONIA *looks towards the door, and gets more and more angry.* TOM'S *head is outside the door; his legs are seen to move convulsively, and the sound of suppressed laughter is heard.*)

GADD (*turning*). Well, well?

TOM (*closing the door sharply, and facing* GADD *with great seriousness*). He is here as the tool of Burroughs.

GADD (*advancing to the* C.). I will receive him.

(TOM *admits* COLPOYS, *who carries a mean-looking "part," and a letter.*)

COLPOYS (*coming* R.C. *after formally bowing to the ladies*). Oh, Gadd, Mr. Burroughs instructs me to offer you this part in the pantomime. (*Handing the part to* GADD.) Demon of Discontent.

(GADD *takes the part and flings it to the ground, down* L. AVONIA *picks it up and reads it.*)

You refuse it?

GADD (*towering over him*). I do. (*With dignity.*) Acquaint Mr. Burroughs with my decision, and add that I hope his pantomime will prove an utterly mirthless one. May Boxing-night, to those unfortunate enough to find themselves in the theatre, long remain a dismal memory; and may succeeding audiences, scanty and dissatisfied——!

(COLPOYS *presents* GADD *with the letter.* GADD *opens it and reads.*)

(*Heavily.*) I leave. The Romeo, the Orlando, the Clifford—(*he sits* L.C.) leaves!

AVONIA (*coming to* GADD, *indicating some lines in the part*). Ferdy, this ain't so bad—(*reading*)

"I'm Discontent! from Orkney's isle to Dover
To make men's bile bile-over I endover——"

GADD. 'Vonia! (*Taking the part from* AVONIA, *with mingled surprise and pleasure.*) Ho, ho! no, that's not bad. (*Reading.*)

"Tempers, though sweet, I whip up to a lather,
Make wives hate husbands, sons wish fathers farther."

'Vonia, there's something to lay hold of here! I'll think this over. (*Rising, addressing* COLPOYS.) Gus, I have thought this over. I play it.

(*They all gather round him, and congratulate him.* AVONIA *embraces and kisses him.*)

TOM.
COLPOYS. } That's right!

ROSE. I'm very pleased, Ferdinand.

AVONIA (*tearfully*). Oh, Ferdy!

GADD (*in high spirits*). Egad, I play it! Gus, I'll stroll back with you to the "Wells."

(TOM *gets up stage* L.C., COLPOYS *goes to door;* AVONIA *gets up* C.)

(*Shaking hands with* ROSE.) Miss Trelawny——! (*Flourishing the part.*) 'Vonia, I see myself in this! (*Kissing her.*) Steak for dinner!

(GADD *and* COLPOYS *go out.* TOM, *now up* C., *shrieks with laughter.*)

AVONIA (R.C., *turning upon him, angrily and volubly*). Yes, I heard you with Colpoys outside that door, if Gadd didn't. It's a pity, Mr. Wrench, you can't find something better to do——!

ROSE (L.C., *pacifically*). Hush, hush, 'Vonia! Tom, assist me with my basket; I'll give 'Vonia her belt——

(TOM *and* ROSE *go behind the curtains and presently emerge carrying the dress-basket which they deposit down* R.C.)

AVONIA (*flouncing across to* L. *front of table*). Making fun of Gadd!—an artist to the roots of his hair! There's more talent in Gadd's little finger——!

ROSE (*rummaging among the contents of the basket*). 'Vonia, 'Vonia!

(TOM *is on his knees, holding the lid up behind the basket.*)

AVONIA (*continuing*). And if Gadd *is* to play a demon in the pantomime, what do *you* figure as, Tom Wrench, among half a dozen other things? Why, as part of a dragon! Yes, and *which end*——? (*She gets* L. *of table.*)

ROSE (*quietly to* TOM). Apologize to 'Vonia at once, Tom.

(TOM *rises and goes* C.)

TOM (*meekly*). Mrs. Gadd, I beg your pardon.

AVONIA (*coming to him and kissing him three sounding kisses*).

Granted, Tom; but you should be a little more considerate——

ROSE (*by basket, holding up the belt*). Here——!

AVONIA (*taking the belt, ecstatically*). Oh, isn't it lovely! Rose, you dear! you sweet thing! (*Singing a few bars of the Jewel song from Faust*—

"Oh what joy—past compare—
These jewels bright to wear——"

then rushing at ROSE *and embracing her.*) I'm going to try my dress on, to show Mrs. Burroughs. Come and help me into it. I'll unlock my door on my side——

(TOM *politely opens the door* R., *for her to pass out.* ROSE *crosses to fire.*)

Thank you, Tom—(*kissing him again*) only you should be more considerate towards Gadd——

(*She disappears.*)

TOM (*calling after her*). I will be; I will—— (*Shutting the door.*) Ha, ha, ha! (*He comes down* R.C.)

ROSE (*smiling*). Hush! Poor 'Vonia! (*Mending the fire.*) Excuse me, Tom—have you a fire upstairs, in your room, to-day?

TOM (R.C.). Er—n—not to-day—(*inspired*) it's Saturday. I never have a fire on a Saturday.

ROSE (*coming to him*). Why not?

TOM (*looking away from her*). Don't know—creatures of habit——

ROSE (*gently touching his coat-sleeve*). Because if you would like to smoke your pipe by my fire while I'm with 'Vonia——

(*The key is heard to turn in the lock of the* C. *door.*)

AVONIA (*from the next room*). It's unlocked.

ROSE. I'm coming.

(*She unbolts the door on her side, and goes into* AVONIA'S *room, shutting the door behind her. A pause*—IMOGEN *to count ten, after* ROSE *shuts the door, before knocking. The lid of the dress-basket is open, showing the contents; a pair of little satin shoes lie at the top.* TOM, *deeply moved, remains in thought, then he sees the basket open. He takes up one of the shoes and presses it to his lips. There is a knock at the door* R. *He returns the shoe to the basket, closes the lid, and walks away to* L.C.)

TOM. Yes?

(*The door opens slightly and* IMOGEN *is heard.*)

IMOGEN (*outside*). Is that you, Wrench?

TOM (*brightening up*). Hullo!

(IMOGEN, *in out-of-door costume, enters breathlessly.*)

IMOGEN (*closing the door—speaking rapidly and excitedly*). Mossop said you were in Rose's room——

TOM (*shaking hands with her*, C.). She'll be here in a few minutes.

IMOGEN. It's you I want. Let me sit down.

TOM (*going to the armchair*, L.). Here——

IMOGEN (*sitting*, R. *of table, panting*). Not near the fire——

TOM (L. *of table*). What's up?

IMOGEN. Oh, Wrench! p'r'aps my fortune's made!

TOM (*quite calmly*). Congratulate you, Jenny.

IMOGEN. Do be quiet; don't make such a racket. You see, things haven't been going at all satisfactorily at the Olympic lately. There's Miss Puddifant——

TOM. I know—no lady.

IMOGEN. *How* do you know?

TOM. Guessed.

IMOGEN. Quite right; and a thousand other annoyances. And at last I took it into my head to consult Mr. Clandon, who married an aunt of mine and lives at Streatham, (*clasping her hands, joyously*) and he'll lend me five hundred pounds.

TOM. What for?

IMOGEN (*extending her arms*). Towards taking a theatre.

TOM (*dubiously*). Five hundred——

IMOGEN. It's all he's good for, and he won't advance that unless I can get a *further* five, or eight, hundred from some other quarter.

TOM. What theatre?

IMOGEN. The *Pantheon* happens to be empty.

TOM. Yes; it's been *that* for the last twenty years.

IMOGEN. Don't throw wet blankets—I mean—(*referring to her tablets, which she carries in her muff*) I've got it all worked out in black and white. There's a deposit required on account of rent—two hundred pounds. Cleaning the theatre—(*looking at* TOM) what do *you* say?

TOM (*leaning towards her*). Cleaning *that* theatre!

IMOGEN. I say, another two hundred.

TOM (*straightening himself*). That would remove the top layer——

IMOGEN. Cost of producing the opening play, five hundred pounds. Balance for emergencies, three hundred. (*To* TOM.) You generally have a balance for emergencies.

TOM. You generally have the emergencies, if not the balance?

IMOGEN. Now the question is, will five hundred produce the play?

TOM. What play?

IMOGEN. Your play.

TOM (*quietly*). My—— (*Leaning towards her.*)

IMOGEN. Your comedy.

TOM (*turning to the fire—in a low voice*). Rubbish!

IMOGEN (*argumentatively*). Well, Mr. Clandon thinks it *isn't*.

(*He faces her sharply.*)

I gave it to him to read, and he—well, he's quite taken with it.

TOM (*walking about, up the stage, his hands in his pockets, his head down, agitatedly*). Clandon—Landon—what's his name——? (*He goes round to* L.C.)

IMOGEN. Tony Clandon—Anthony Clandon——

TOM (*choking*). He's a—he's a——

IMOGEN. He's a hop-merchant.

TOM. No he's not—(*sitting on the sofa, leaning his head on his hands*) he's a stunner.

IMOGEN (*rising*). So you grasp the position. Theatre—manageress—author—play, found; and eight hundred pounds *wanted*!

TOM. Oh, lord!

IMOGEN. Who's got it?

TOM (*rising—wildly*). The Queen's got it! Miss Burdett-Coutts has got it! (*He gets to* R.C.)

IMOGEN (C.). Don't be a fool, Wrench. Do you remember old Mr. Morfew, of Duncan Terrace? He used to take great interest in us all at the "Wells." *He* has money.

TOM. He has gout; we don't see him now.

IMOGEN. Gout!—how lucky! That means he's at home. Will you run round to Duncan Terrace——?

TOM (*looking down at his clothes*). I!

IMOGEN. Nonsense, Wrench; we're not asking him to advance money on your clothes.

TOM. The clothes are the man, Jenny.

IMOGEN. And the woman——?

TOM. The face is the woman.

IMOGEN (*facing audience*). I'll go! Is my face good enough?

TOM (*enthusiastically*). I should say so!

IMOGEN (*taking his hands*). Ha, ha! it has been in my possession longer than you have had your oldest coat, Tom!

TOM. Make haste, Jenny! (*He gets over to up* L.C.)

IMOGEN (*running up to the door* R.). Oh, it will last till I get to Duncan Terrace. (*Turning.*) Tom, you may have to read your play to Mr. Morfew. Have you another copy? Uncle Clandon has mine.

TOM (*holding his head*). I think I have—I don't know——

IMOGEN. Look for it! find it! If Morfew wants to hear it, we must strike while the iron's hot.

TOM. While the gold's hot!

IMOGEN.
TOM. } Ha, ha, ha!

(MRS. MOSSOP *enters, door* R., *showing some signs of excitement.*)

IMOGEN (*pushing her aside*). Oh, get out of the way, Mrs. Mossop——

(IMOGEN *departs.*)

MRS. MOSSOP (*up* C.). Upon my——! (*To* TOM.) A visitor for Miss Trelawny! Where's Miss Trelawny?

TOM (*up* L.C.). With Mrs. Gadd. (*She is going up* C. *as he catches her by the wrist and turns her towards him.*) Mossop!

MRS. MOSSOP. Don't bother me now——

TOM. Mossop, the apartments vacated by the Telfers! Dare to let 'em without giving me the preference.

MRS. MOSSOP. You!

TOM (*seizing her hands and swinging her round. He gets to* R. *of her*). I may be wealthy, sweet Rebecca! (*Embracing her.*) I may be rich and honoured!

MRS. MOSSOP. Oh, have done! (*Releasing herself and setting her cap and apron straight.*) My lodgers do take such liberties——

TOM (*at the door, grandly*). Beccy, half a scuttle of coal, to start with.

(*He goes out, leaving the door slightly open.*)

MRS. MOSSOP (*knocking at the* C. *door*). Miss Trelawny, my dear! Miss Trelawny!

(*The* C. *door opens, a few inches.*)

ROSE (*looking out*). Why, what a clatter you and Mr. Wrench have been making——!

MRS. MOSSOP (*beckoning her mysteriously*). Come here, dear.

ROSE (*closing the* C. *door, and entering the room wonderingly*) Eh? (*She comes down a little* L.C.)

MRS. MOSSOP (*in awe*). Sir William Gower!

ROSE. Sir William!

MRS. MOSSOP. Don't be vexed with me. "I'll see if she's at home," I said. "Oh yes, woman, Miss Trelawny's at home," said he, and hobbled straight in. I've shut him in the Telfers' room——

(*There are three distinct raps, with a stick, at the door* R.)

ROSE.
MRS. MOSSOP. } Oh—h!

ROSE (*faintly*). Open it. (*Up above table* L.C.)

(MRS. MOSSOP, *after some hesitation, opens the door, and* SIR WILLIAM *enters and comes* C. *He is feebler, more decrepit, than when last seen. He wears a plaid about his shoulders and walks with the aid of a stick.*)

MRS. MOSSOP (*at the door*). Ah, and a sweet thing Miss Trelawny is——!

SIR WILLIAM (C., *turning to her*). Are you a relative?

MRS. MOSSOP. No, I am *not* a relative——

SIR WILLIAM. Go.

(*She departs ; he closes the door with the end of his stick.*)

(*Returning to* C.—*facing* ROSE ; *he stands looking at her for a moment, then quietly removes his hat.*) My mind is not commonly a wavering one, Miss Trelawny, but it has taken me some time—months—to decide upon calling on ye.

ROSE (L.C., *above table*). Won't you sit down ?

(*He goes to front of basket, tapping it with his stick as he goes.*)

SIR WILLIAM (*after a pause of hesitation, sitting upon the dress-basket*). Ugh !

ROSE (*with quiet dignity*). Have we no chairs ? Do we lack chairs here, Sir William ?

(*He gives her a quick, keen look, then rises and walks to the fire, putting hat upon table above fireplace* L.)

SIR WILLIAM (*turning suddenly, bringing his stick down upon the table with violence*). My grandson ! my grandson ! Where is he ? (*Leaves stick on table.*)

ROSE (C.). Arthur—— !

SIR WILLIAM (*taking off gloves—irritably*). I had but one.

ROSE. Isn't he—in Cavendish Square—— ?

SIR WILLIAM (*getting front of table*). Isn't he in Cavendish Square ! No, he is not in Cavendish Square, as you know well.

ROSE. Oh, I *don't* know——

SIR WILLIAM. Tsch !

ROSE (R.C.). When did he leave you ?

SIR WILLIAM. Tsch !

ROSE. When ?

SIR WILLIAM. He made his escape during the night, twenty-second of August last—(*pointing his finger at her*) as you know well.

ROSE. Sir William, I assure you——

SIR WILLIAM (L.C.). Tsch ! (*Taking off his gloves.*) How often does he write to ye ?

ROSE. He does not write to me. He did write day after day, two or three times a day, for about a week. That was in June, when I came back here. (*With drooping head.*) He never writes now.

SIR WILLIAM. Visits ye—— ?

ROSE. No.

SIR WILLIAM. Comes troubadouring—— ?

ROSE. No, no, no. I have not seen him since that night. I refused to see him—— (*With a catch in her breath.*) Why, he may be—— !

SIR WILLIAM (*fumbling in his pocket*). Ah, but he's not. (*Throws gloves on table.*) He's alive ; (*producing a small packet of letters*) Arthur's alive, (*advancing to her*) and full of his tricks still. His great-aunt Trafalgar receives a letter from him once a fortnight, posted in London——

ROSE (*holding out her hand for the letters*). Oh——!

SIR WILLIAM (*putting them behind his back*). Hey!

ROSE (*faintly*). I thought you wished me to read them.

(*He yields them to her grudgingly.*)

(*Taking his hand and bending over it.*) Ah, thank you.

SIR WILLIAM (*withdrawing his hand with a look of disrelish*). What are ye doing, madam? What are ye doing?

(*He sits*, R. *of table, producing his snuff-box; she sits, upon the basket, facing him, and opens the packet of letters.*)

ROSE (*reading a letter*). "To reassure you as to my well-being, I cause this to be posted in London by a friend——"

SIR WILLIAM (*pointing a finger at her again, accusingly*). A friend!

ROSE (*looking up, with simple pride*). He would never call me *that*. (*Reading.*) "I am in good bodily health, and as contented as a man can be who has lost the woman he loves, and will love till his dying day——" Ah——!

SIR WILLIAM. Read no more! Return them to me!

(*She holds the letters to her breast.*)

Give them to me, ma'am!

(*Slowly rising, she restores the letters, meekly, holding the letters on fingers of both hands, so that he can take them easily.*)

(*Peering up into her face.*) What's come to ye? You are not so much of a vixen as you were.

ROSE (*shaking her head*). No.

SIR WILLIAM (*suspiciously*). Less of the devil——?

ROSE (*her eyes cast down*). Sir William, I am sorry for having been a vixen, and for all my unruly conduct, in Cavendish Square. I humbly beg your, and Miss Gower's, forgiveness.

SIR WILLIAM (*taking snuff, uncomfortably, he turns and looks at her*). Pi—i—i—sh! extraordinary change.

ROSE. Aren't *you* changed, Sir William, now that you have lost him?

SIR WILLIAM. I!

ROSE. Don't you love him now, the more?

(*His head droops a little, and his hands wander to the brooch which secures his plaid.*)

Let me take your shawl from you. You would catch cold when you go out——

(*He allows her to remove the plaid, protesting during the process.*)

SIR WILLIAM. I'll not trouble ye, ma'am. Much obleeged to ye, but I'll not trouble ye. (*Rising and picking up stick.*) I'll not trouble ye——

(*He walks away to the fireplace, and then up* L.C. *She folds the plaid and lays it upon the sofa.*)

(*Looking round—in an altered tone.*) My dear, gipsying doesn't seem to be such a good trade with ye, as it used to be by all accounts—— (*He is up* L.C. *above table.*)

(*The* C. *door opens and* AVONIA *enters boldly, in the dress of a burlesque prince—cotton-velvet shirt, edged with bullion trimming, a cap, white tights, ankle boots, etc.*)

AVONIA (*unconsciously*). How's this, Rose——? (*Going to* ROSE, R.C.)

SIR WILLIAM. Ah—h—h—h!

ROSE (*above basket* R.C.). Oh, go away, 'Vonia!

AVONIA. Sir Gower! (*To* SIR WILLIAM.) Good morning.

(*She withdraws,* C.)

SIR WILLIAM (*pacing the room, up the stage—again very violent*). Yes! and these are the associates you would have tempted my boy —my grandson—to herd with! (*Flourishing his stick.*) Ah—h—h—h! (*He goes a little up* C.)

ROSE (*sitting upon the basket, facing up the stage—weakly*). That young lady doesn't live in that attire. She is preparing for the pantomime——

SIR WILLIAM (*standing over her*). And now he's gone; lured away, I suspect, by one of ye—(*pointing to the* C. *door*) by one of these harridans——!

(AVONIA *reappears defiantly.*)

AVONIA (*up* L.C.). Look here, Sir Gower——

ROSE (*rising*). Go, 'Vonia! (*Her hand to her heart.*)

AVONIA (*to* SIR WILLIAM). We've met before, if you remember, in Cavendish Square——

ROSE (*sitting again, helplessly*). Oh, Mrs. Gadd——!

SIR WILLIAM. Mistress! a married lady!

AVONIA. Yes, I spent some of my honeymoon at your house——

SIR WILLIAM. What!

AVONIA. Excuse my dress; it's all in the way of my business. (*Coming down,* L. *of table.*) Just one word about Rose. (*She raps on the table.*)

ROSE. Please, 'Vonia——!

AVONIA (*to* SIR WILLIAM, *who is glaring at her in horror*). Now, there's nothing to stare at, Sir Gower. If you must look anywhere in particular, look at that poor thing. A nice predicament you've brought her to!

SIR WILLIAM (C.). Sir——! (*Correcting himself.*) Madam!

AVONIA. You've brought her to beggary, amongst you! You've broken her heart; and, what's worse, you've made her genteel. She can't act, since she left your mansion; she can only mope about the stage with her eyes fixed, like a person in a dream—dreaming of him, I suppose, and of what it is to be a lady.

(SIR WILLIAM *gets above table to* R. *of it.*)

And first she's put upon half-salary; and then, to-day, she gets the sack—(*she leans over table to him*) the entire sack, Sir Gower! So there's nothing left for her but to starve, or to make artificial flowers. Miss Trelawny I'm speaking of! (*Crossing to* ROSE, *who rises and stands above basket, and embracing her.*) Our Rose! our Trelawny! (*To* ROSE, *breaking down.*) Excuse me for interfering, ducky. (*Retiring, in tears.*) Good day, Sir Gower.

(*She goes out,* C. *door.* SIR WILLIAM *puts stick quietly on table and stands* L.C. *in front of chair.*)

SIR WILLIAM (*after a pause, to* ROSE). Is this—the case?

ROSE (*standing,* R.C.—*in a low voice*). Yes. As you have noticed, fortune has turned against me, rather.

SIR WILLIAM (*penitently*). I—I'm sorry, ma'am. I—I believe ye've kept your word to us concerning Arthur. I—I——

ROSE (*not heeding him, looking before her, dreamily*). My mother knew how fickle fortune could be to us gipsies. One of the greatest actors that ever lived warned her of that——

SIR WILLIAM. Miss Gower will also feel extremely—extremely——

ROSE (*as before*). Kean once warned mother of that.

SIR WILLIAM (*in an altered tone*). Kean? Which Kean?

ROSE. Edmund Kean. My mother acted with Edmund Kean, when she was a girl.

SIR WILLIAM (*approaching her slowly, speaking in a queer voice*). With Kean? with Kean!

ROSE. Yes.

SIR WILLIAM (*at her side, in a whisper*). My dear, I—*I've* seen Edmund Kean.

ROSE. Yes?

SIR WILLIAM. A young man then, I was; quite different from the man I am now—impulsive, excitable. Kean! (*Drawing a deep breath.*) Ah, he was a *splendid* gipsy!

ROSE (*looking down at the dress-basket*). I've a little fillet in there that my mother wore as Cordelia to Kean's Lear——

SIR WILLIAM. I may have seen your mother also. I was somewhat different in those days——

ROSE (*kneeling at the basket and opening it*). And the Order and chain, and the sword, he wore in Richard. He gave them to my father; I've always prized them.

(*She drags to the surface a chain with an Order attached to it, and a sword-belt and sword—all very theatrical and tawdry—and a little gold fillet.*)

(*Handing him the chain.*) That's the Order.

SIR WILLIAM (*handling it tenderly*). Kean! God bless me!

ROSE (*holding up the fillet*). My poor mother's fillet.

SIR WILLIAM (*looking at it*). I may have seen her. (*Thoughtfully, gazing in front.*) I was a young man then. (*Looking at* ROSE *steadily.*) Put it on, my dear.

(*She looks at him inquiringly and crosses to the mirror* L. *and puts on the fillet.*)

(*Examining the Order.*) Lord bless us! How he stirred me! how he——!

(*He puts the chain over his shoulders.* ROSE *turns to him.*)

ROSE (*advancing to him*). There!

SIR WILLIAM (*looking at her*). Cordelia! Cordelia—with Kean!

ROSE (*adjusting the chain upon him*). This should hang so. (*Returning to front of the basket and taking up the sword-belt and sword.*) Look!

SIR WILLIAM (*handling them*). Kean! (*To her, in a whisper.*) I'll tell ye! I'll tell ye! When I saw him as Richard—I was young and a fool—(*he goes a step or two to* L., *then returns to her*) I'll tell ye—he almost fired me with an ambition to—to—— (*Fumbling with the belt.*) How did he carry this?

ROSE (*fastening the belt, with the sword, round him*). In this way—— (*She gets* L. *of him as she does so.*)

SIR WILLIAM. Ah!

(*He paces the stage, growling and muttering, and walking with a limp and one shoulder hunched. He goes down round basket, up to* R.C., *muttering,* "Now is the winter of our discontent," *etc. She watches him, seriously, standing* L.)

(*Up* R., *partly to himself.*) Ah! he was a little man too! (*Going up* L., *muttering, then returning to* C. *and drawing sword.*) I remember him, as if it were last night! I remember—— (*Pausing,* C., *sword in hand, looking at her fixedly.*) My dear, your prospects in life have been injured by your unhappy acquaintanceship with my grandson.

ROSE (*gazing into the fire*). Poor Arthur's prospects in life—what of them?

SIR WILLIAM (*testily, flourishing sword*). Tsch, tsch, tsch!

ROSE. If I knew where he is——!

SIR WILLIAM. Miss Trelawny, if you cannot act, you cannot earn your living. (*Taps on table with point of sword.*)

ROSE. How is he earning *his* living?

SIR WILLIAM. And if you cannot earn your living, you must be provided for.

ROSE (*turning to him*). Provided for ?

SIR WILLIAM (R.C.). Miss Gower was kind enough to bring me here in a cab. She and I will discuss plans for making provision for ye, while driving home.

ROSE (*advancing to him*). Oh, I beg you will do no such thing, Sir William.

SIR WILLIAM (R.C.). Hey !

ROSE. I could not accept any help from you or Miss Gower.

SIR WILLIAM. You must ! You shall !

ROSE. I will not.

SIR WILLIAM (*touching the Order and the sword*). Ah—— ! Yes, I—I'll buy these of ye, my dear——

ROSE. Oh, no, no ! not for hundreds of pounds ! Please take them off !

(*There is a hurried knocking at the door* R.)

SIR WILLIAM (*startled*). Who's that ? (*Struggling with the chain and belt.*) Remove these—— !

(*The handle is heard to rattle.* SIR WILLIAM *disappears behind the curtains.* ROSE *closes the curtains, removes fillet from her head, puts it in the basket, closes the lid, and gets away to up* L.C. *as* IMOGEN *opens the door and looks in.*)

IMOGEN (*seeing only* ROSE, *and coming to her and embracing her*). Rose darling, where is Tom Wrench ?

ROSE. He was here not long since——

IMOGEN (*going to the door and calling, desperately*). Tom ! Tom Wrench ! Mr. Wrench !

ROSE (*up* L.C., *above table*). Is anything amiss ?

IMOGEN (*shrilly*). Tom !

ROSE. Imogen !

IMOGEN (*returning to* ROSE). Oh, my dear, forgive my agitation—— !

(TOM *enters, buoyantly, flourishing the manuscript of his play.*)

TOM. I've found it ! At the bottom of a box—" deeper than did ever plummet sound——" !

(ROSE *goes down* L.)

(*To* IMOGEN.) Eh ? What's the matter ?

IMOGEN. Oh, Tom, old Mr. Morfew—— !

TOM (*blankly*). Isn't he willing—— ?

IMOGEN (*with a gesture of despair*). I don't know. He's dead.

TOM. No !

IMOGEN. Three weeks ago. (*Coming to down* R.C.) Oh, what a chance he has missed !

(TOM *crosses and bangs his manuscript down upon the table savagely.*)

ROSE (*down* L.C.). What is it, Tom? Imogen, what is it?

IMOGEN (*going up* R., *and pacing the stage*). I can think of no one else——

TOM. Done again!

IMOGEN (*up* R.). We shall lose it, of course——

ROSE. Lose what?

TOM (C.). The opportunity—her opportunity, *my* opportunity, *your* opportunity, Rose.

ROSE (*coming a little* L.C.). *My* opportunity, Tom?

TOM (*pointing to the manuscript*). My play—my comedy—

(IMOGEN *works quietly across to down* L.)

—my youngest born! Jenny has a theatre—could have one—has five hundred towards it, put down by a man who believes in my comedy, God bless him—! (*with a break in his voice—going down* R.C.) the only fellow who has ever believed——!

ROSE (*going* C.). Oh, Tom! (*turning to* IMOGEN, *who is now* L.) oh, Imogen!

IMOGEN. My dear, five hundred! We want another five, at least.

ROSE. Another five!

IMOGEN. Or eight.

TOM. And you are to play the part of Dora. Isn't she, Jenny —I mean, wasn't she?

IMOGEN. Certainly. Just the sort of simple little Miss you *could* play now, Rose. And we thought that old Mr. Morfew would help us in the speculation. Speculation!—it's a dead certainty!

TOM. *Dead* certainty? Poor Morfew! (*He sits on basket facing audience.*)

IMOGEN. And here we are, stuck fast——!

TOM. And they'll expect me to rehearse that dragon to-morrow with enthusiasm.

ROSE (*putting her arm round his shoulder*). Never mind, Tom.

TOM. No, I won't—(*taking her hand*) Oh, Rose—! (*looking up at her*) oh, Dora——!

(SIR WILLIAM, *divested of his theatrical trappings, comes from behind the curtain.*)

IMOGEN. Oh——!

TOM (*rising and getting to* R.). Eh?

ROSE (*retreating to* R. *a little*). Sir William Gower, Tom.

SIR WILLIAM (C., *to* TOM). I had no wish to be disturbed, sir, and I withdrew (*bowing to* IMOGEN) when that lady entered the room. I have been a party, it appears, to a consultation upon a matter of business. (*To* TOM.) Do I understand, sir, that you have been defeated in some project which would have served the interests of Miss Trelawny? (*He puts his hand on hers.*)

TOM. Y—y—yes, sir.

SIR WILLIAM. Mr. Wicks——

TOM. Wrench——

SIR WILLIAM. Tsch! Sir, it would give me pleasure—it would give my grandson, Mr. Arthur Gower, pleasure—to be able to aid Miss Trelawny at the present moment.

(TOM *and* IMOGEN *look at each other.*)

TOM (*down* R.). S—s—sir William, w—w—would you like to hear my play—— ?

SIR WILLIAM (*sharply*). Hey! (*Looking round.*) Ho, ho!

TOM. My comedy?

SIR WILLIAM (*cunningly*). So ye think I might be induced to fill the office ye designed for the late Mr.—Mr.——

IMOGEN. Morfew.

SIR WILLIAM. Morfew, eh?

TOM. N—n—no, sir.

SIR WILLIAM. No! no!

IMOGEN (*shrilly*). Yes!

SIR WILLIAM (*after a short pause, quietly*). Read your play, sir. (*Pointing to the chair above table.*) Sit down.

(SIR WILLIAM *moves chair* R. *of table up a little and* TOM, *amazed, crosses to above table and sits.*)

(*To* ROSE *and* IMOGEN.) Sit down.

(MISS GOWER'S *voice is heard outside the door* R.)

MISS GOWER (*outside*). William!

(ROSE *opens the door;* MISS GOWER *enters.*)

(C., *faintly.*) Oh, William, what has become of you? Has anything dreadful happened?

SIR WILLIAM (*by chair* R. *of table*). Sit down, Trafalgar. This gentleman is about to read a comedy. A cheer! (*Testily.*) Are there no cheers here?

(ROSE *brings the chair from up* R., *and places it for* MISS GOWER *beside* SIR WILLIAM'S *chair.*)

Sit down.

MISS GOWER (*sitting, bewildered*). William, is all this—quite—— ?

SIR WILLIAM (L.C. *by table*). Yes, Trafalgar, quite in place—quite in place——

(IMOGEN *sits* L. ROSE *pulls the dress-basket round, to face the audience, as* COLPOYS *and* GADD *swagger in, at the door* R., COLPOYS *smoking a pipe,* GADD *a large cigar.* GADD *shuts the door.*)

(L.C., *to* TOM, *referring to* GADD *and* COLPOYS.) Friends of yours?

TOM. Yes, Sir William.

SIR WILLIAM (*to* GADD *and* COLPOYS). Sit down. (*Imperatively.*) Sit down and be silent!

(GADD *and* COLPOYS *seat themselves upon the sofa, like men in a dream.* ROSE *sits on the dress-basket.*)

AVONIA (*opening the* C. *door slightly—in an anxious voice*). Rose——!

SIR WILLIAM (*rapping on table*). Come in, ma'am, come in!

(AVONIA *enters, coming down to* ROSE. *A cloak is now attached to the shoulders of* AVONIA'S *dress.*)

(*To* AVONIA.) Sit down, sit down, ma'am.

(AVONIA *sits beside* ROSE, *next to* MISS GOWER.)

MISS GOWER (*using her smelling-bottle—in horror*). Oh—h—h—h!

SIR WILLIAM (*restraining her*). Quite in place, Trafalgar; quite in place. (*He sits—to* TOM.) Now, sir!

TOM (*opening his manuscript and reading*). "Life, a comedy, by Thomas Wrench——"

The CURTAIN *falls.*

ACT IV

(As altered for the revival of the play at the Victoria Theatre—the "Old Vic"—in 1925.)

ACT IV

The SCENE *represents the stage of a theatre, the footlights and proscenium arch of the actual stage being the proscenium arch and the footlights of the mimic stage. At the back is an old and worn pair of flats dimly picturing a baronial hall. Some odd pieces of scenery are piled against the flats. On the* L. *runs a brick wall in which, up* L., *is a doorway admitting to the Green-room. Down* L., *set obliquely to face the stage, is the prompt-table. A chair is on either side of it. Down* R., *not far from the proscenium arch, stands a large throne-chair with a gilt frame and red velvet seat, now much dilapidated, and* L.C., *close to the flats at the back, there are a " property " stool, a table and a chair, all of a similar style to the throne-chair and in like condition. In the middle of the stage, as if placed there for the purpose of rehearsal, are another table and chair. On this table is a work-basket containing a ball of wool and a couple of knitting-needles ; and on the prompt-table there is a book. A faded and ragged carpet of green baize covers the floor of the stage.*

The wings and borders, and any other scenic appointments which may be shown, should suggest by their shabbiness a theatre fallen into decay. The light is a dismal one, but it is relieved by a shaft of sunlight entering through a window in the flies.

Down L., *in front of the proscenium arch, there is a flight of wooden steps, fixed temporarily to enable the stage-manager to leave the stage at certain times and direct the rehearsal from the stalls.*

(See Plan of the Scene, and refer to the original prompt-book for details of " business," etc.)

MRS. TELFER *is seated upon the throne-chair in an attitude of dejection.* TELFER *enters from the Green-room.*

TELFER (*coming to her*). Is that you, Violet ?

MRS. TELFER. Is the reading over ?

TELFER. Almost. My part is confined to the latter 'alf of the second act ; so being close to the Green-room door, (*with a sigh*) I stole away.

MRS. TELFER. It affords you no opportunity, James ?

TELFER (C., *shaking his head*). A mere fragment.

MRS. TELFER (*rising*). Well, but a few good speeches to a man of your stamp——

TELFER. Yes, but this is so line-y, Violet ; so very line-y. And what d'ye think the character is described as ?

MRS. TELFER. What ?

TELFER. "An old, stagey, out-of-date actor."

(*They stand looking at each other for a moment, silently.*)

MRS. TELFER (*falteringly*). Will you—be able—to get near it, James?

TELFER (*looking away from her*). I daresay——

MRS. TELFER (*laying a hand upon his shoulder*). That's all right, then.

TELFER. And you—what have they called you for, if you're not in the play? They 'ave not dared to suggest understudy?

MRS. TELFER (*playing with her fingers*). They don't ask me to act at all, James.

TELFER. Don't ask you——!

MRS. TELFER. Miss Parrott offers me the position of Wardrobe-mistress.

TELFER. Violet——!

MRS. TELFER. Hush!

TELFER. Let us both go home.

MRS. TELFER (*restraining him*). No, let us remain. We've been idle six months, and I can't bear to see you without your watch and all your comforts about you.

TELFER (*pointing towards the Green-room*). And so this new-fangled stuff, and these dandified people, are to push us, and such as us, from our stools!

MRS. TELFER. Yes, James, just as some other new fashion will, in course of time, push *them* from their stools.

(*From the Green-room comes the sound of a slight clapping of hands, followed by a murmur of voices.* IMOGEN, *elaborately dressed, enters from the Green-room and goes leisurely to the prompt-table. She is followed by* TOM, *manuscript in hand, smarter than usual in appearance; and he by* O'DWYER—*an excitable Irishman of about forty, with an extravagant head of hair—who carries a small bundle of "parts" in brown-paper covers.* TOM *and* O'DWYER *join* IMOGEN.)

O'DWYER (*to* TOM). Mr. Wrench, I congratulate ye; I have that honour, sir. Your piece will do, sir; it will take the town, mark me.

TOM. Thank you, O'Dwyer.

IMOGEN. Look at the sunshine! There's a good omen, at any rate.

O'DWYER (*between* TOM *and* IMOGEN). Oh, sunshine's nothing. (*To* TOM.) But did ye observe the gloom on their faces whilst ye were readin'?

IMOGEN (*anxiously*). Yes, they did look glum.

O'DWYER. Glum!—it might have been a funeral! There's a healthy prognostication for ye, if ye loike! It's infallible.

(*A keen-faced gentleman and a lady enter, from the Green-room, and stroll across the stage to up* R., *where they lean against the wings and talk. Then two young gentlemen enter and loiter about at the back.* ROSE *follows, coming down* C.

Note.—The actors and the actress appearing for the first time in this act, as members of the Pantheon Company, are outwardly greatly superior to the GADDS, *the* TELFERS *and* COLPOYS.)

ROSE (*shaking hands with* TELFER). Why didn't you sit near me, Mr. Telfer? (*Crossing to* MRS. TELFER *and kissing her.*) Fancy our being together again, and at the West End! (*To* TELFER.) Do you like the play?

TELFER. Like it! There's not a speech in it, my dear—not a real *speech*; nothing to dig your teeth into——

O'DWYER (*allotting the parts, under the direction of* TOM *and* IMOGEN). Mr. Mortimer!

(*One of the young gentlemen advances and receives his part from* O'DWYER, *and retires, reading it, to second entrance* L.)

Mr. Denzil!

(*The keen-faced gentleman who is standing up* R. *takes his part, then joins* IMOGEN *and talks to her. The lady now has something to say to the solitary young gentleman at the back.*)

TOM (*to* O'DWYER, *quietly, handing him a part*). Miss Brewster.

O'DWYER (*beckoning to the lady, who does not observe him*). Come here, my love.

TOM (*to* O'DWYER). No, no, O'Dwyer—not your "love."

O'DWYER (*perplexed*). Not?

TOM. No.

O'DWYER. No?

TOM. Why, you are meeting her this morning for the first time.

O'DWYER. That's true enough. (*Approaching the lady and handing her the part.*) Miss Brewster.

THE LADY. Much obliged.

O'DWYER (*aside to her*). It'll fit ye like a glove, darlin'.

(*The lady sits at the table at the back, conning her part.* O'DWYER *returns to the prompt-table.*)

TELFER (*to* ROSE). Your lover in the play? Which of these young sparks plays your lover—Harold or Gerald——?

ROSE. Gerald. I don't know. There are some people not here to-day, I believe.

O'DWYER. Mr. Hunston!

(*The second young gentleman advances, receives his part, and rejoins the other young gentleman.*)

ROSE. Not that young man, I hope. Isn't he a little bandy?

TELFER. One of the finest Macduffs I ever fought with was bow-legged.

O'DWYER. Mr. Kelfer!

TOM (*to* O'DWYER). No, no—Telfer.

O'DWYER. Telfer.

(TELFER *draws himself erect, puts his hand in his breast, but otherwise remains stationary.*)

MRS. TELFER (*anxiously*). That's you, James.

O'DWYER. Come on, Mr. Telfer! Look alive, sir!

TOM (*to* O'DWYER). Sssh, sssh, sssh! don't, don't——!

(TELFER *advances to the prompt-table, slowly. He receives his part from* O'DWYER.)

(*To* TELFER, *awkwardly.*) I—I hope the little part of Poggs appeals to you, Mr. Telfer. Only a sketch, of course; but there was nothing else—quite—in your——

TELFER. Nothing? To whose share does the Earl fall?

TOM. Oh, Mr. Denzil plays Lord Parracourt.

TELFER. Denzil? I've never 'eard of 'im. Will you get to me to-day?

TOM. We—we expect to do so.

TELFER. Very well. (*Stiffly.*) Let me be called in the street.

(*He stalks away up* R.)

MRS. TELFER (*relieved*). Thank heaven! I was afraid James would break out.

ROSE (*to* MRS. TELFER). But you, dear Mrs. Telfer—you weren't at the reading—what are *you* cast for?

MRS. TELFER. I? (*Wiping away a tear.*) I am the Wardrobe-mistress of this theatre.

ROSE. You! (*Embracing her.*) Oh! oh!

MRS. TELFER (*composing herself*). Miss Trelawny—Rose—my child, if we are set to scrub a floor—and we may come to that yet—let us make up our minds to scrub it legitimately—with dignity——

(*She disappears, second entrance* R., *and is seen no more.*)

O'DWYER. Miss Trelawny! Come here, my de——

TOM (*to* O'DWYER). Hush!

O'DWYER. Miss Trelawny!

(ROSE *receives her part from* O'DWYER *and, after a word or two with* TOM *and* IMOGEN, *joins the two young gentlemen. The lady who has been seated at the back now rises and meets the keen-faced gentleman who has finished his conversation with* IMOGEN.)

THE LADY (*to the keen-faced gentleman*). I say, Mr. Denzil, who plays Gerald?

THE GENTLEMAN (*down* R.C.). Gerald?

THE LADY. The man I have my scene with in the third act—the hero——

THE GENTLEMAN. Oh, a young gentleman from the country, I understand.

THE LADY. From the country!

THE GENTLEMAN. He is coming up by train this morning, Miss Parrott tells me; from Bath or somewhere——

THE LADY. Well, whoever he is, if he can't play that scene with me decently, my part's not worth rags.

TOM (*to* IMOGEN, *who is sitting at the prompt-table*). Er—h'm—shall we begin, Miss Parrott?

IMOGEN. Certainly, Mr. Wrench.

TOM. We'll begin, O'Dwyer.

(*The lady titters at some remark from the keen-faced gentleman.*)

O'DWYER (*coming down the stage, violently*). Clear the stage there! I'll not have it! Upon my honour, this is the noisiest theatre I've ever set foot in!

(*The stage is cleared, the characters, other than* O'DWYER, IMOGEN *and* TOM, *disappearing into the Green-room.*)

I can't hear myself speak for all the riot and confusion!

TOM (*to* O'DWYER). My dear O'Dwyer, there is *no* riot, there is *no* confusion——

IMOGEN (*to* O'DWYER). Except the riot and confusion *you* are making.

TOM. You know, you're admirably earnest, O'Dwyer, but a little excitable.

O'DWYER (*calming himself*). Oh, I beg your pardon, I'm sure. (*Emphatically.*) My system is, begin as ye mean to go on.

IMOGEN. But we *don't* mean to go on like that.

TOM. Of course not; of course not. Now, let me see—(*pointing to the table in the* C.) we shall want another chair here.

O'DWYER. Another chair?

TOM. A garden chair.

O'DWYER (*excitably*). Another chair! Now then, another chair! Properties! where are ye? do ye hear me callin'? must I raise my voice to ye——?

(*He rushes away, second entrance* R.)

IMOGEN (*to* TOM). Phew! where did you get *him* from?

TOM (*wiping his brow*). Known Michael for years—most capable, invaluable fellow——

IMOGEN (*simply*). I wish he was dead.

TOM. So do I.

(O'DWYER *returns, carrying a light chair.*)

Well, where's the property man?

O'DWYER (*pleasantly*). It's all right, now. He's gone to dinner

TOM (*placing the chair in position*). Ah, then he'll be back some time during the afternoon. (*Looking about him.*) That will do. (*Taking up his manuscript.*) Call—haven't you engaged a call-boy yet, O'Dwyer?

O'DWYER. I have, sir, and the best in London.

IMOGEN. Where is he?

O'DWYER. He has sint an apology for his non-attindance.

IMOGEN. Oh——!

O'DWYER. A sad case, ma'am! He's buryin' his wife.

TOM. Wife!

IMOGEN. The call-boy!

TOM. What's his age?

O'DWYER. Ye see, he happens to be an elder brother of my own——

IMOGEN. }
TOM. } Oh, lord!

TOM. Never mind! Let's get on! Call Miss—(*looking towards* R.) is that the Hall-Keeper?

(*A man, suggesting by his appearance that he is the* HALL-KEEPER, *presents himself, second entrance* R., *with a card in his hand.*)

O'DWYER (*furiously*). Now then! Are we to be continually interrupted in this fashion? Have I, or have I not, given strict orders that nobody whatever——?

TOM. Hush, hush! see whose card it is; give me the card——

O'DWYER (*handing the card to* TOM). Ah, I'll make rules here. In a week's time you'll not know this for the same theatre——

(TOM *has passed the card to* IMOGEN *without looking at it.*)

IMOGEN (*staring at it blankly*). Oh——!

TOM (*to her*). Eh?

IMOGEN. Sir William!

TOM. Sir William!

IMOGEN. What can he want? what shall we do?

TOM (*after referring to his watch—to the* HALL-KEEPER). Bring this gentleman on to the stage.

(*The* HALL-KEEPER *withdraws.*)

(*To* O'DWYER.) Make yourself scarce for a few moments, O'Dwyer. Some private business——

O'DWYER. All right. I've plenty to occupy me. I'll begin to frame those rules——

(*He disappears, second entrance* L.)

IMOGEN (*to* TOM). Not here——

TOM (*to* IMOGEN). The boy can't arrive for another twenty minutes. Besides, we must, sooner or later, accept responsibility for our act.

IMOGEN (*leaning upon his arm*). Heavens! I foretold this!

TOM (*grimly*). I know—"said so all along."

IMOGEN. If he should withdraw his capital!

TOM (*with clenched hands*). At least, that would enable me to write a melodrama.

IMOGEN. Why?

TOM. I should then understand the motives and the springs of Crime!

(*The* HALL-KEEPER *reappears, showing the way to* SIR WILLIAM GOWER. SIR WILLIAM'S *hat is drawn down over his eyes, and the rest of his face is almost entirely concealed by his plaid. The* HALL-KEEPER *withdraws.*)

(*Receiving* SIR WILLIAM.) How d'ye do, Sir William?

SIR WILLIAM (*giving him two fingers—with a grunt*). Ugh!

TOM. These are odd surroundings for you to find yourself in——

(IMOGEN *advances.*)

Miss Parrott——

SIR WILLIAM (*going to her—giving her two fingers*). Good morning, ma'am.

IMOGEN. This is perfectly delightful.

SIR WILLIAM. What is?

IMOGEN (*faintly*). Your visit.

SIR WILLIAM. Ugh! (*Weakly.*) Give me a cheer. (*Looking about him.*) Have ye no cheers here?

TOM. Yes.

(TOM *places the throne-chair nearer to* SIR WILLIAM. SIR WILLIAM *sinks into it.*)

SIR WILLIAM. Thank ye; much obleeged. (*To* IMOGEN.) Sit.

(IMOGEN *hurriedly fetches the stool from the back and seats herself beside the throne-chair.*)

(*Producing his snuff-box.*) You are astonished at seeing me here, I daresay?

TOM (*on his* R., *boldly*). Not at all.

SIR WILLIAM (*glancing at* TOM). Addressing the lady. (*To* IMOGEN.) You are surprised to see me?

IMOGEN. Very.

SIR WILLIAM (*to* TOM). Ah!

(TOM *retreats, getting behind* SIR WILLIAM'S *chair and looking down upon him.*)

The truth is, I am beginning to regret my association with ye.

IMOGEN (*her hand to her heart*). Oh—h—h—h!

TOM (*under his breath*). Oh! (*Holding his fist over* SIR WILLIAM'S *head.*) Oh—h—h—h!

IMOGEN (*pitcously*). You—you don't propose to withdraw your capital, Sir William?

SIR WILLIAM. That would be a breach of faith, ma'am——

IMOGEN. Ah!

TOM (*walking about, jauntily*). Ha!

IMOGEN (*seizing* SIR WILLIAM'S *hand*). Friend!

SIR WILLIAM (*withdrawing his hand sharply*). I'll thank ye not to repeat that action, ma'am. But I—I have been slightly indisposed since I made your acqueentance in Clerkenwell; I find myself unable to sleep at night. (*To* TOM.) That comedy of yours—it buzzes continually in my head, sir.

TOM (R.C.). It was written with such an intention, Sir William—to buzz in people's heads.

SIR WILLIAM. Ah, I'll take care ye don't read me another, Mr. Wicks; at any rate, another which contains a character resembling a member of my family—a *late* member of my family. I don't relish being reminded of late members of my family in this way, and being kept awake at night, thinking—turning over in my mind——

IMOGEN (*soothingly*). Of course not.

SIR WILLIAM (*taking snuff*). Pa—a—a—h! pi—i—i—sh! When I saw Kean, as Richard, he reminded me of no member of my family. Shakespeare knew better than that, Mr. Wicks. (*To* IMOGEN.) And therefore, ma'am, upon receiving your letter last night, acqueenting me with your intention to commence rehearsing your comedy—(*glancing at* TOM) *his* comedy——

IMOGEN (*softly*). *Our* comedy——

SIR WILLIAM. Ugh!—to-day at noon, I determined to present myself here and request to be allowed to—to——

TOM (*sharply*). To watch the rehearsal?

SIR WILLIAM. The rehearsal of those episodes in your comedy which remind me of a member of my family—a *late* member.

IMOGEN (*constrainedly*). Oh, certainly——

TOM (*firmly*). By all means.

SIR WILLIAM (*rising, assisted by* TOM). I don't wish to be steered at by any of your—what d'ye call 'em?—your gipsy crew——

TOM. Ladies and Gentlemen of the Company, we call 'em.

SIR WILLIAM (*tartly*). I don't care what ye call 'em.

(TOM *restores the throne-chair to its former position.*)

Put me into a curtained box, where I can hear, and see, and not be seen; and when I've heard and seen enough, I'll return home—and—and obtain a little sleep; and to-morrow I shall be well enough to sit in Court again.

TOM (*up* L., *calling*). Mr. O'Dwyer——

(O'DWYER *appears;* TOM *speaks a word or two to him, and hands him the manuscript of the play.*)

IMOGEN (*to* SIR WILLIAM, *falteringly*). And if you are pleased with what you see this morning, perhaps you will attend another—— ?

SIR WILLIAM (*angrily*). Not I. After to-day I wash my hands of ye. What do plays and players do, coming into my head, disturbing my repose! (*More composedly, to* TOM, *who has returned to his side.*) Your comedy has merit, sir. You call it *Life*. There is a character in it—a young man—not unlike life—not unlike a late member of my family. Obleege me with your arm. My box, sir—my box——

(TOM *leads* SIR WILLIAM *to down* L.)

TOM (*to* O'DWYER). Begin rehearsal. Begin rehearsal! Call Miss Trelawny!

(TOM *and* SIR WILLIAM *disappear down* L.)

O'DWYER. Miss Trelawny! Miss Trelawny! (*Rushing to up* L.C.) Miss Trelawny! how long am I to stand here shoutin' myself hoarse—— ?

(ROSE *appears* L.)

ROSE (*gently*). Am I called ?

O'DWYER (*instantly calm*). You are, darlin'.

(O'DWYER *stands* C., *book in hand.* IMOGEN *and* ROSE *stand together near prompt-table. The other members of the company come from the Green-room and stand up* L., *watching the rehearsal.*)

Now then! (*Reading from the manuscript.*) "At the opening of the play Peggy and Dora are discovered——" Who's Peggy? (*Excitedly.*) Where's Peggy? Am I to—— ?

IMOGEN. Here I am! here I am! I am Peggy.

O'DWYER (*calm*). Of course ye are, lovey—ma'am, I should say——

IMOGEN. Yes, you should.

O'DWYER. "Peggy is seated upon the Right, Dora on the Left——"

(ROSE *and* IMOGEN *seat themselves accordingly.*)

(*In a difficulty.*) No—Peggy on the Left, Dora on the Right. (*Violently.*) This is the worst written scrip I've ever held in my hand——

(ROSE *and* IMOGEN *change places.*)

So horribly scrawled over, and interlined, and—no—I was quite correct. Peggy is on the Right, and Dora is on the Left.

(IMOGEN *and* ROSE *again change seats.*)

(*Reading from the manuscript.*) "Peggy is engaged in—in——" I can't decipher it. A scrip like this is a disgrace to any well-conducted theatre. (*To* IMOGEN.) I don't know what you're doin'. "Dora is—is——" (*To* ROSE.) You are also doin' something or another. Now then! When the curtain rises, you are discovered, both of ye, employed in the way described——

(TOM *returns.*)

Ah, here ye are! (*Resigning the manuscript to* TOM, *and pointing out a passage.*) I've got it smooth as far as there.

TOM. Thank you.

O'DWYER (*seating himself at prompt-table*). You're welcome.

TOM (C., *to* ROSE *and* IMOGEN). Ah, you're not in your right positions. Change places, please.

(IMOGEN *and* ROSE *change seats once more.* O'DWYER *rises and goes off second entrance* L.)

O'DWYER (*out of sight, violently*). A scrip like that's a scandal! If there's a livin' soul that can read bad handwriting, I am that man! But of all the——!

TOM. Hush, hush! Mr. O'Dwyer!

O'DWYER (*returning to his chair*). Here.

TOM (*taking the book from the prompt-table and handing it to* IMOGEN). You are reading.

O'DWYER (*sotto voce*). I thought so.

TOM (*to* ROSE). You are working.

O'DWYER. Working.

TOM (*pointing to the basket on the* C. *table*). There are your needles and wool.

(ROSE *takes the wool and the needles out of the basket.*)

(*Taking the ball of wool from her and placing it on the ground in the* C. *of the stage.*) You have allowed the ball of wool to roll from your lap on to the grass. (*Hurrying down the wooden steps and directing the rehearsal from the front row of the stalls.*) The curtain rises. (*To* IMOGEN.) Miss Parrott——

IMOGEN (*referring to her part*). What do I say?

TOM. Nothing—you yawn.

IMOGEN (*yawning, in a perfunctory way*). Oh—h!

TOM. As if you meant it, of course.

IMOGEN. Well, of course.

O'DWYER (*jumping up*). This sort of thing. (*Yawning extravagantly.*) He—oh!

TOM (*irritably*). Thank you, O'Dwyer; thank you.

O'DWYER (*sitting again*). You're welcome.

TOM (*to* ROSE). You speak.

ROSE (*reading from her part—retaining the needles and the end of the wool*). "What are you reading, Miss Chaffinch?"

IMOGEN (*reading from her part*). "A novel."

ROSE. "And what is the name of it?"

Imogen. "*The Seasons.*"

Rose. "Why is it called that?"

Imogen. "Because all the people in it do seasonable things."

Rose. "For instance——?"

Imogen. "In the Spring, fall in love."

Rose. "In the Summer?"

Imogen. "Become engaged. Delightful!"

Rose. "Autumn?"

Imogen. "Marry. Heavenly!"

Rose. "Winter?"

Imogen. "Quarrel. Ha, ha, ha!"

Tom (*to* Imogen). Close the book—with a bang——

(*During all the above* Tom, *manuscript in hand, moves from one side of the stalls to the other, gesticulating in the manner of a conductor of an orchestra.*)

O'Dwyer (*bringing his hands together sharply by way of suggestion*). Bang!

Tom (*irritably*). Yes, yes, O'Dwyer. (*To* Imogen.) Now rise——

O'Dwyer. Up ye get!

Tom. And walk about, discontentedly.

Imogen (*walking about*). "I've nothing to do; let's tell each other our ages."

Rose. "I am nineteen."

Tom (*to* Imogen). In a loud whisper——

Imogen. "I am twenty-two."

O'Dwyer (*rising, and speaking to* Tom *across the footlights*). Now, hadn't ye better make that *six*-and-twenty?

Imogen (*coming forward with asperity*). Why? why?

Tom. No, no, certainly not. Go on.

Imogen (*angrily*). Not till Mr. O'Dwyer retires into his corner.

Tom. O'Dwyer——

(O'Dwyer, *with the air of martyrdom, disappears down* L.)

(*At the prompt-table, to* Rose.) You speak.

Rose. "I shall think, and feel, the same when I am twenty-two, I am sure. I shall never wish to marry."

Tom (*returning to the stage and summoning the keen-faced gentleman*). Mr. Denzil.

O'Dwyer (*putting his head round the corner*). Mr. Denzil!

(*The keen-faced gentleman comes forward, reading his part, and meets* Imogen, C.)

The Gentleman (*speaking in the tones of an old man*). "Ah, Miss Peggy!"

Tom (*down* C., *to* Rose). Rise, Miss Trelawny.

O'Dwyer (*his head again appearing*). Rise, darlin'!

(ROSE *rises.*)

THE GENTLEMAN (*to* IMOGEN). "Your bravura has just arrived from London. Lady McArchie wishes you to try it over."

IMOGEN (*taking his arm*). "Delighted, Lord Parracourt. (*To* ROSE.) Miss Harrington, bring your work indoors and hear me squall."

(IMOGEN *and the keen-faced gentleman indicate that they go off* L. *He rejoins his companions ; she returns to the prompt-table.*)

ROSE. "Why do Miss Chaffinch and her girl-friends talk of nothing, think of nothing apparently, but marriage ? Ought a woman to make marriage the great object of life ? Can there be no other ? I wonder——"

(*She goes off* L., *the wool trailing after her, and disappears into the Green-room. The ball of wool remains in the* C. *of the stage.*)

TOM (*reading from his manuscript*). "The piano is heard ; and Peggy's voice singing. Gerald enters——"

IMOGEN (*clutching* TOM'S *arm*). There——!

TOM. Ah, yes, here is Mr. Gordon.

(ARTHUR *appears, second entrance* R., *in a travelling coat.* TOM *and* IMOGEN *hasten to him and shake hands with him vigorously.*)

How are you ?

IMOGEN (*nervously*). How are you ?

ARTHUR (*breathlessly, getting between the two*). Miss Parrott ! Mr. Wrench ! forgive me if I am late ; my cab-horse galloped from the station——

TOM. We had just reached your entrance. Have you read your part over ?

ARTHUR. Read it ! (*Taking it from his pocket.*) I know every word of it ! It has made my journey from Bristol like a flight through the air ! Why, Mr. Wrench, (*turning over the leaves of his part*) some of this is almost *me* !

TOM }
IMOGEN } (*nervously*). Ha, ha, ha !

TOM. Come ! you enter ! (*Pointing to down* R.) There ! (*Running down the wooden steps.*) You stroll on, looking about you ! (*In the stalls again.*) Now, Mr. Gordon !

ARTHUR (*advancing from down* R. *to the* C. *of the stage, occasionally glancing at his part*). "A pretty place. I am glad I left the carriage at the lodge and walked through the grounds."

(*There is an exclamation, proceeding from* SIR WILLIAM, *who, seated behind a curtain, is in the stage-box in the auditorium, and the sound of the overturning of a chair.*)

IMOGEN. Oh !

O'DWYER (*appearing, looking into the auditorium*). What's that? This is the noisiest theatre I've ever set foot in——!

TOM. Don't heed it! (*To* ARTHUR.) Go on, Mr. Gordon.

ARTHUR. "Somebody singing. A girl's voice. Lord Parracourt made no mention of anybody but his hostess—the dry, Scotch widow. (*Picking up the ball of wool.*) This is Lady McArchie's, I'll be bound. The very colour suggests spectacles and iron-grey curls——"

TOM. Dora returns. (*Calling.*) Dora!

O'DWYER. Dora! where are ye?

THE GENTLEMEN (*going towards the Green-room door*). Dora! Dora!

(ROSE *appears in the wings, up* L.)

ROSE (*to* TOM). I'm sorry.

TOM. Go on, please!

(*There is another sound, nearer the stage, of the overturning of some object.*)

O'DWYER. What——?

TOM. Don't heed it!

ROSE (*coming face to face with* ARTHUR). Oh——!

ARTHUR. Rose!

TOM. Go on, Mr. Gordon!

ARTHUR (*to* ROSE, *holding out the ball of wool*). "I beg your pardon—are you looking for this?"

ROSE. "Yes, I—I—I——" Oh, Mr. Gower, why are you here?

ARTHUR. Don't you know?

ROSE. No.

ARTHUR. Why, Miss Trelawny, I am trying to be—what you are.

ROSE. What I am——?

ARTHUR. Yes—a gipsy.

ROSE. A gipsy—a gip—— (*Dropping her head upon his breast.*) Oh, Arthur!

(SIR WILLIAM *totters on from down* L.)

SIR WILLIAM. Arthur!

ARTHUR (*going to him*). Grandfather!

O'DWYER (*indignantly*). Upon my soul——!

TOM. Leave the stage, O'Dwyer!

(O'DWYER *vanishes down* L. IMOGEN *goes to the members of the company at the back and talks to them; gradually they withdraw into the Green-room.* ROSE *retreats up* R.C. *as* TOM *hurriedly returns to the stage.*)

SIR WILLIAM. What's this? What is it——?

Arthur (*bewildered*). Sir, I—I—you—and—and Rose—are the last persons I expected to meet here——

Sir William. Ah—h—h—h!

Arthur. Perhaps you have both already learnt, from Mr. Wrench or Miss Parrott, that I have—become—a gipsy, sir?

Sir William. Not *I*; (*pointing to* Tom *and* Imogen) these—these people have thought it decent to allow me to make the discovery for myself.

(*He sinks into the throne-chair.* Tom *crosses to him.* Rose *goes to* Arthur.)

Tom (*to* Sir William). Sir William, the secret of your grandson's choice of a profession——

Sir William (*scornfully*). Profession!

Tom. Was one that I was pledged to keep as long as it was possible to do so. And pray remember that your attendance here this morning is entirely your own act. It was our intention——

Sir William (*struggling to his feet*). Where is the door? the way to the door?

Tom. And let me beg you to understand this, Sir William—that Miss Trelawny was, till a moment ago, as ignorant as yourself of Mr. Arthur Gower's doings, of his movements, of his whereabouts. She would never have thrown herself in his way, in this manner. Whatever conspiracy——

Sir William. Conspiracy! The right word—conspiracy!

Tom. Whatever conspiracy there has been is my own—to bring these two young people together again, to make them happy——

(Rose *holds out her hand to* Tom; *he takes it. They are joined by* Imogen, *who comes down* L.)

Sir William (*looking about him*). The door! the door!

Arthur (*going to* Sir William). Grandfather, may I, when rehearsal is over, venture to call in Cavendish Square——?

Sir William. Call——!

Arthur. Just to see Aunt Trafalgar, sir? I hope Aunt Trafalgar is well, sir.

Sir William (*with a slight change of tone*). Your Great-Aunt Trafalgar? Ugh, yes, I suppose she will consent to see ye——

Arthur. Ah, sir——!

Sir William. But *I* shall be out; *I* shall not be within doors.

Arthur. Then, if Aunt Trafalgar will receive me, sir, do you think I may be allowed to—to bring Miss Trelawny with me——?

Sir William. What! ha, I perceive you have already acquired the impudence of your vagabond class, sir; (*advancing to* C.) the brazen effrontery of a set of——!

Rose (*facing him*). Forgive him! forgive him! Oh, Sir William, why may not Arthur become, some day, a *splendid* gipsy?

Sir William. Eh?

Rose. Like——

Sir William (*peering into her face*). Like——?

Rose. Like——

Tom. Yes, sir, a gipsy, though of a different order from the old order which is departing—a gipsy of the new school!

Sir William (*to* Rose). Well, Miss Gower is a weak, foolish lady; for aught I know she may allow this young man to—to—take ye——

Imogen (*advancing to* l.c.). I would accompany Rose, of course, Sir William.

Sir William (*tartly*). Thank ye, ma'am. (*Turning.*) I'll go to my carriage.

Arthur. Sir, if you have the carriage here, and if you would have the patience to sit out the rest of the rehearsal, we might return with you to Cavendish Square.

Sir William (*choking*). Oh—h—h—h!

Arthur. Grandfather, we are not rich people, and a cab to us——

Sir William (*exhausted*). Arthur——!

Tom. Sir William will return to his box! (*Going to the* l.) O'Dwyer!

Sir William (*protesting weakly*). No, sir! no!

(O'Dwyer *appears.*)

Tom. Mr. O'Dwyer, escort Sir William Gower to his box.

(Arthur *leads* Sir William *to* O'Dwyer, Sir William *still uttering protests.* Rose *and* Imogen *embrace,* r.c.)

O'Dwyer (*giving an arm to* Sir William). Lean on me, sir! heavily, sir——!

Tom. Shall we proceed with the rehearsal, Sir William, or wait till you are seated?

Sir William (*violently*). Wait! Confound ye, d'ye think I want to remain here all day!

(Sir William *and* O'Dwyer *disappear down* l.)

Tom (*coming to* c., *with* Arthur *on his* l.—*wildly*). Go on with the rehearsal! Mr. Gordon and Miss Rose Trelawny! Miss Trelawny!

(Rose *goes to him, on his* r.)

Trelawny—late of the "Wells"! Let us—let——

(*Gripping* Arthur's *hand tightly, he bows his head upon* Rose's *shoulder.*)

Oh, my dears—! let us—get on with the rehearsal——!

Sir William *shows himself in the front of the stage-box as*

The Curtain *falls.*

FURNITURE AND PROPERTY PLOT

ACT I

Scenery

Round table, 7 feet in diameter.
Large pattern carpet.
Black door furniture.
Walls papered with bold flower-pattern paper—not flock.
Sideboard-cupboards painted *very* light oak, and grained.
Two very high sash windows R., to work; exterior backing.
The door down L. opens on and up stage: a landing is seen outside—marble block pattern paper.
Plain ceiling.
Doors and windows painted to match sideboard.

Properties

Venetian blinds and lace curtains on brass poles and curtain-hooks to windows.
A horsehair and mahogany chair in each window.
Piano and stool between windows R. On desk of piano an open copy of "Ever of Thee"; on top of piano a quantity of old music, some old playbooks, a basket of wax fruit under glass, a wig-block on which is a cavalier ringlet-wig (iron grey) and a jewelled sword.
On wall above piano hangs an oval mirror in gilt frame, and above the mirror an engraving in maple frame.
In corner up R. two or three old swords.
On sideboard R., decanters of port and sherry; glass knife-rests; glass-cloth; knife-box containing 4 carving-knives and forks; 12 table knives and forks with black handles; 12 dessertspoons and forks, silver-plated; bread on bread-dish; bread-knife; 12 glass tumblers, and two large white beer-jugs.
Above the sideboard hangs an oil portrait in gilt frame, supposed to be "Mrs. Mossop"; another over sideboard L., "Mr. Mossop."
Fireirons and fender, and grate filled with paper shavings, paper roses and gilt cuttings.
Skin hearthrug.
Handsome mantelpiece, with glass gas-brackets on each side of the overmantel with lustres. On the mantel, a large black marble clock; pair of lustres; vases containing paper spills to light pipes. Tall, handsome looking-glass (gilt frame, covered with yellow gauze) with reflection of ornaments painted.
White bell-pulls R. and L. of mantel.
R. of mantel, hanging on wall, a pipe-rack with clay pipes; on L. of mante, a quantity of play-bills of the period. On each side of the mirror hang daguerreotypes.
On sideboard L., 2 cruets; pickles in cut-glass jars; flowers in glass bowls, and dishes for table decoration—these flowers are thrown at Rose during her speech—and a quantity of plates.
In corner, leaning against wall on sideboard, two combat swords, and on the floor in corner, more swords and walking-sticks.

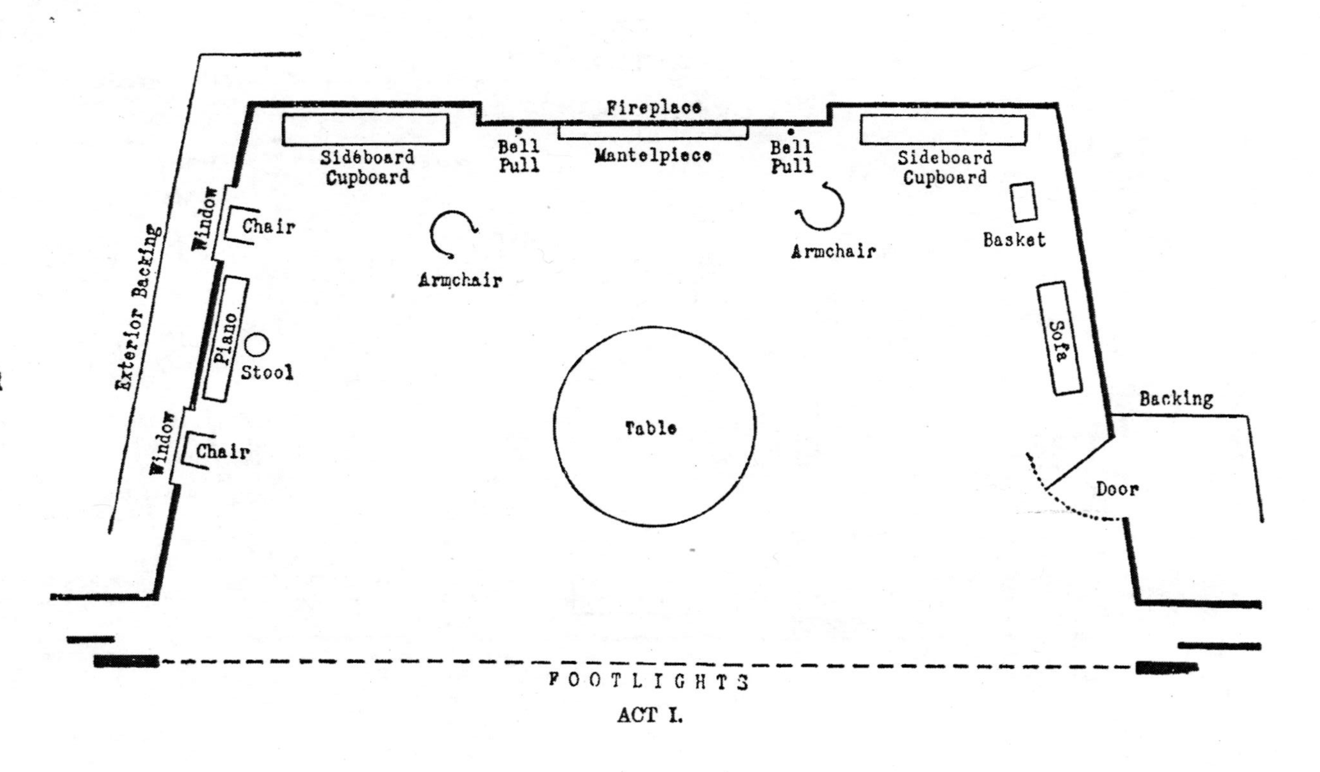
Fireplace
Mantelpiece
Bell Pull
Bell Pull
Sidéboard Cupboard
Sideboard Cupboard
Armchair
Armchair
Basket
Sofa
Backing
Door
Table
Window
Chair
Piano
Stool
Window
Chair
Exterior Backing
FOOTLIGHTS

ACT I.

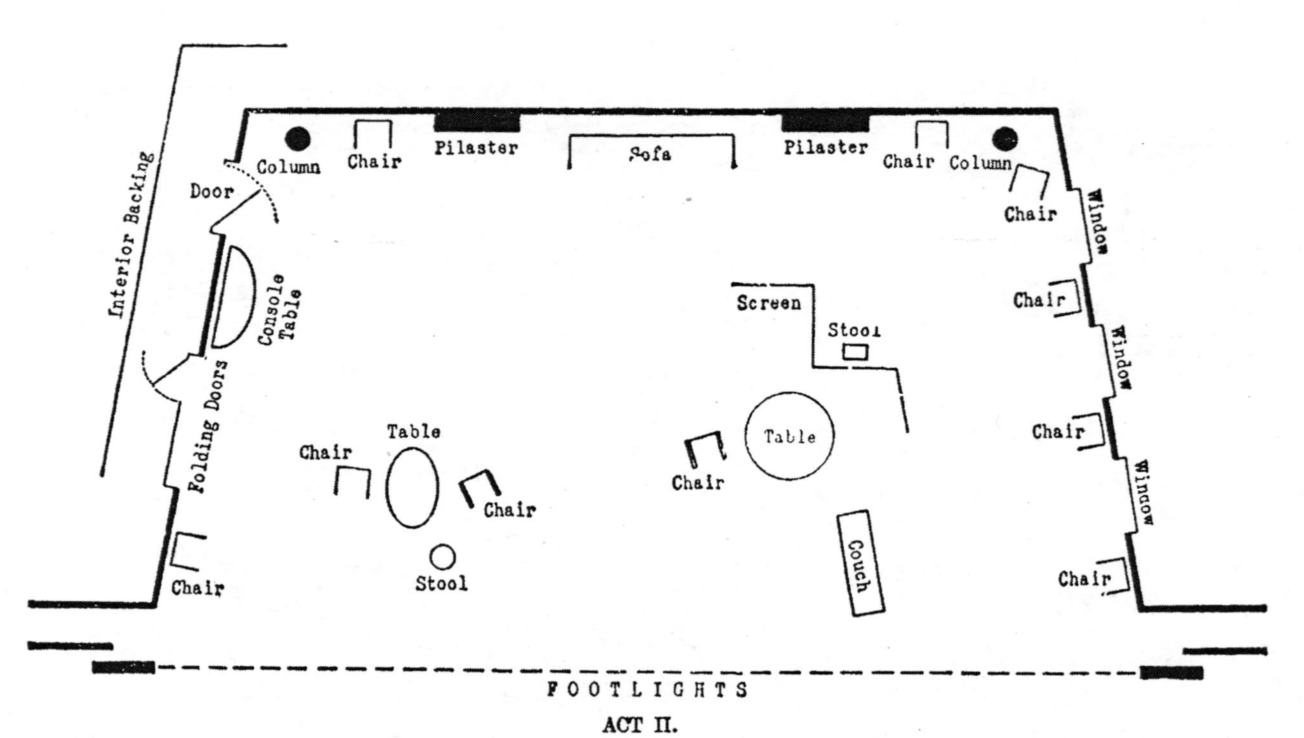
Interior Backing
Door
Column
Chair
Pilaster
Sofa
Pilaster
Chair
Column
Chair
Window
Console Table
Chair
Screen
Stool
Window
Folding Doors
Table
Chair
Chair
Table
Chair
Chair
Window
Couch
Chair
Stool
Chair
FOOTLIGHTS

ACT II.

On wall L. and above door, there are engravings in maple frames. A large black trunk or basket with name painted in faded lettering, "Miss Violet Sylvester, Theatre Royal, Drury Lane."

Large armchair (horsehair and mahogany) each side of fireplace, with large woollen antimacassar.

Horsehair and mahogany sofa L.: on this, a white satin bodice, some old play-books, lights, pillow covered in rep, flowers, theatrical hat, etc., etc. Under sofa, old satin slippers, playbooks, etc.

Outside, door L., a piece of oil-cloth, and a mat.

Ready off R., a street-door knocker.

Hand Properties

ABLETT.—White cotton gloves (2 "lefts").

6 chairs of various kinds, ready for him to carry on.

Beer ready to put into jugs when he brings them off.

Large tray, on which is a pigeon-pie, a ham and a tongue, for him to carry on.

IMOGEN *and* AVONIA.—Parasols.

TOM.—Scissors.

GADD.—Benefit bill.

MRS. MOSSOP.—Large tray with joint of beef, a chicken and two vegetable-dishes of hot potatoes.

SARAH.—Old kitchen Windsor chair.

ACT II

Scenery

Walls painted dull green; the dado and pictures dull grey; there is a deep cornice of the same colour.

L., 3 glazed windows, recessed, showing square outside.

Ceiling a dull colour.

R., folding-doors in three folds, but only top fold used; it opens off stage. These doors are recessed.

Up R., a single door opening on and down stage; a dark backing to this door.

Between this door and the folding-doors a console table and a mirror.

R. and L. of pilasters, at back, hang full-length portraits in gilt frames of "Sir William Gower" in his Vice-Chancellor's robes and wig, and of "Miss Gower" in lady's dress of the period.

Above upper door R., a large oval picture.

Properties

Green rep curtains to windows L., and gilt cornices. Curtain bands and hooks; curtains to work.

In lower window L., a card-table, below it, an occasional chair, and above it 3 others. The card-table and chairs are brought to L.C., during the act, and eventually overturned.

Up L., marble pedestal with bust.

The portraits of the Gowers hang on the back wall.

The sofa at back is two-headed, and has a silk patchwork cushion and woollen antimacassars on each head. A large brown skin rug lies in front of it.

Up R., marble pedestal with bust.

On console table R., there stands an old-fashioned lamp, lighted.

Large brown skin rug in front of folding-doors.

The easy chair, L. of table down R., has a low seat and no arms.

L.C. there is a sofa, with head up stage, and silk patchwork cushion.

Above sofa, an oval table with very handsomely worked cover, with bullion fringe; on table a tall old-fashioned lamp, lighted, to be turned out at cue; an alabaster ornament under glass shade; 2 packs of cards, and card-counters in worked beaded bag.

R. of this table a lady's easy chair.
The screen is fourfold, of mahogany and rep; a footstool is behind it.

Hand Properties

Charles.—Two silver-plated candlesticks, with lighted candles and green shades, ready off R.
Limp note; house lantern.
Avonia.—Wet hat and umbrella.
Gadd.—Wooden pipe and coins.
Colpoys.—Coins.
Sir William.—Snuff-box; silver-plated bedroom candlestick and lighted candle, and walking-stick, ready R.
Rose.—Plate of biscuits, and silver salver with decanter of sherry and wine-glasses ready for Charles, off R.
Also—Piano off R., with copy of "Ever of Thee."
Lightning, rain, thunder, ready L.
Bells to ring off stage, and a wood crash when the table is upset.
Old-fashioned barrel-organ, to play off L. at cue.

ACT III

Scenery

The scene represents a "bed-sitting-room."
Wallpaper poor but bright.
Doors, skirtings, etc., stone colour.
R., a door opening on and down stage; outside this door, staircase backing.
Between C. and R.C., at back, a recessed door, opening off; practical lock, with key outside and small practical bell inside. Outside this door, interior backing to represent another room.
Down L., a fireplace.
Plain ceiling.

Properties

Carpet poor, with bold pattern.
Sofa, R., mahogany and horsehair, with crochet-work antimacassar, and some books upon it.
Under sofa, some ladies' boots and 2 blue bonnet-boxes.
On wall above sofa hangs a bookcase.
Cheap engravings are seen about the walls.
Above door R., a bedroom chair; in corner up R., a mahogany corner-cupboard.
Up the stage R.C., a small chest of drawers, the top covered with a clean white toilet-cover; on this, a basin and jug, soap-dish, tooth-brush dish, water-bottle and glass.
Above the chest of drawers hangs a small looking-glass, and in front of it stands a threefold screen (flowers and scrap-covered). To the L. of this 3 pegs on the wall, with ladies' dresses.
Lock and key and bolt on door C., to work; also lock to work on door R.
L. of C. door, up stage, some more pegs.
In L. corner is a single bedstead, the bedding neat and scrupulously clean.
Against wall L., below the bed, a clean-looking basket containing wardrobe, etc., placed there before the act, as follows: Jewelled belt (worn as Ophelia) plain fillet (worn as Cordelia), jewelled order with wild boar hanging from it, jewelled sword and chain (supposed to have been worn by Kean as "Richard III"), and a pair of white satin ladies' slippers.
From back wall, by C. door, to wall L., below basket, about 7 feet high, runs a stout cord, and curtains to work. When drawn, the curtains mask the bed and basket. The curtains are of a dull, faded red, with black velvet band for trimming.

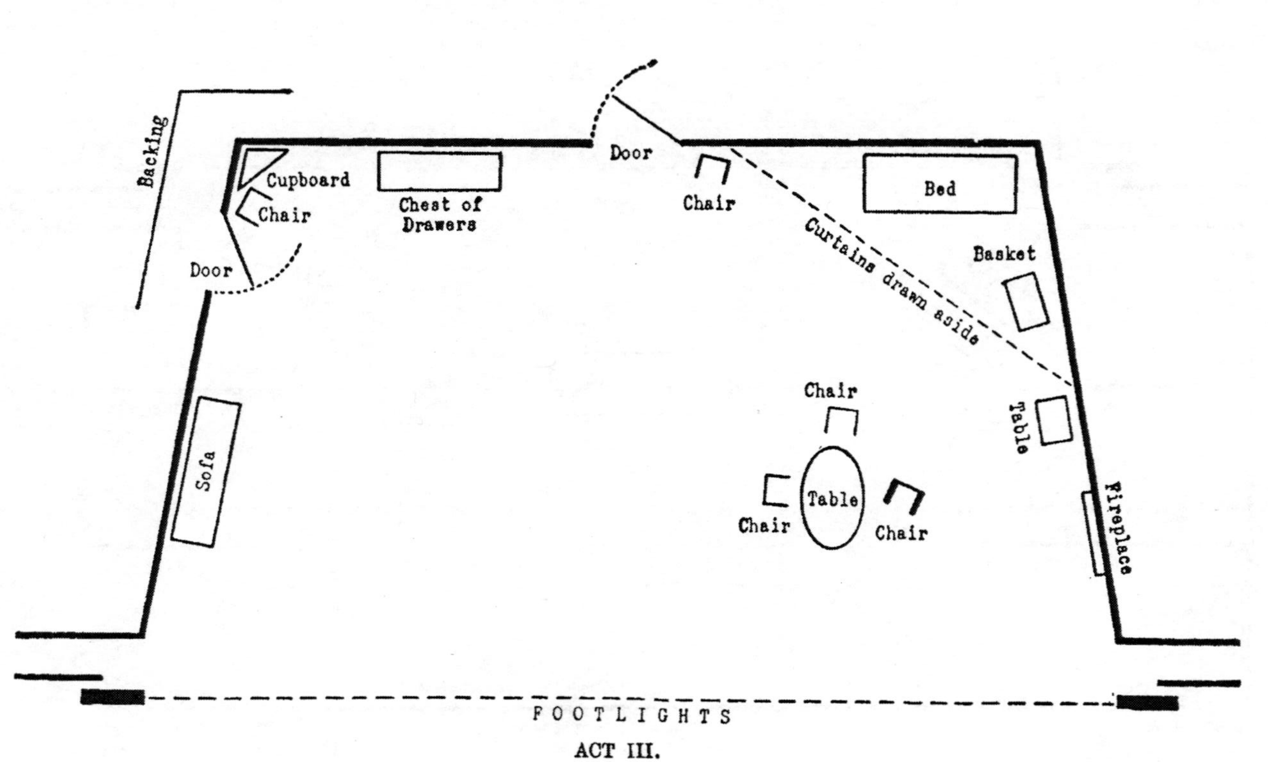
Backing
Backing
Cupboard
Chair
Chest of Drawers
Door
Door
Chair
Bed
Curtains drawn aside
Basket
Table
Chair
Table
Chair
Chair
Sofa
Fireplace
FOOTLIGHTS

ACT III.

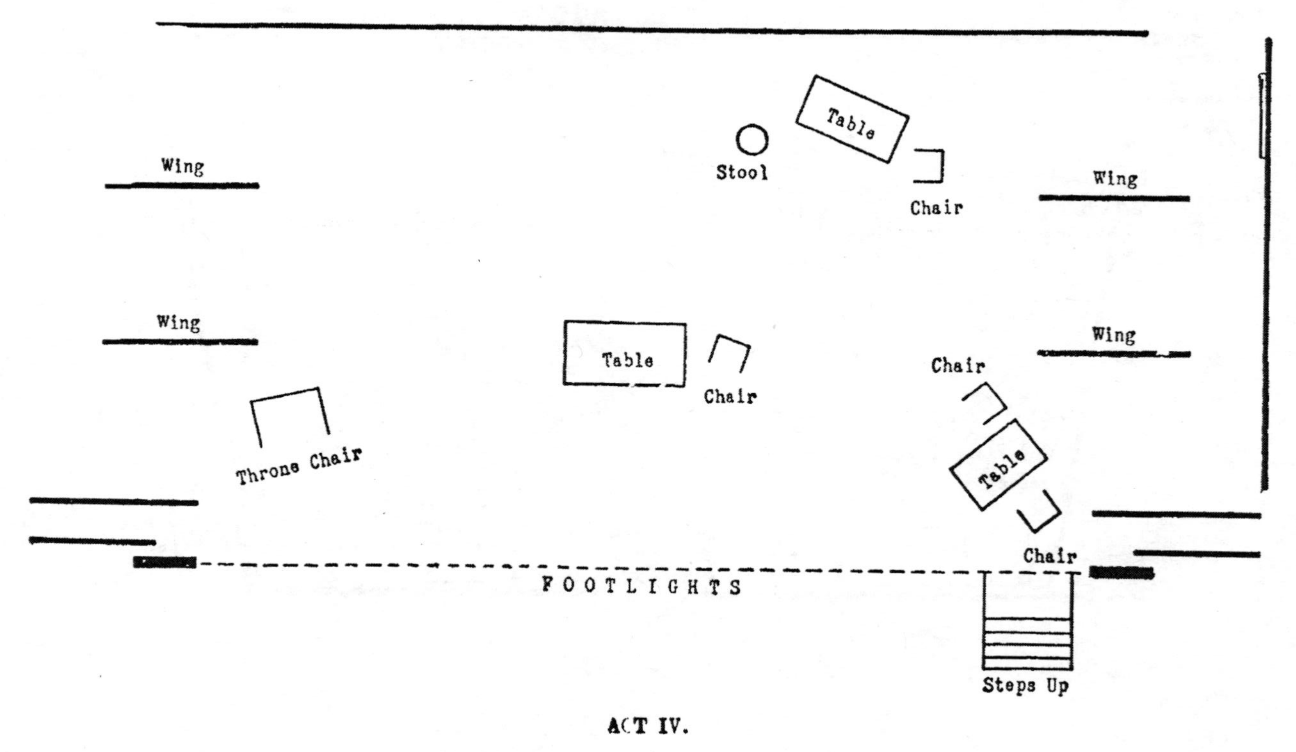
Wing
Stool
Table
Chair
Wing
Wing
Table
Chair
Chair
Wing
Throne Chair
Table
Chair
FOOTLIGHTS
Steps Up

ACT IV.

Between curtain and fireplace L., a small work-table.

The fire is lighted in old-fashioned stove, with hob and kettle; nursery fender and irons; mantelpiece with a poor clock, china ornaments, looking-glass, etc.

Below fireplace, a coal-scuttle, and black bell-pull.

Black door furniture.

A bright but poor hearthrug.

In front of fire an old-fashioned armchair; to R. of this, an oval table covered with a very dingy cloth, and on this an inkstand, blotter, pens, paper and envelopes, and a duster and dusting brush. Bedroom chairs R. of and above this table.

Outside C. door, a table and 2 chairs and a picture hung on backing, to convey the idea of another room.

HAND PROPERTIES

AVONIA.—Curling-tongs.

TOM.—Bright table-cover, and written letter in pocket; manuscripts of play, written, ready R.

ROSE.—Reticule and umbrella.

IMOGEN.—Muff and tablets.

COLPOYS. One-leaf-part in brown paper, and letter in envelope; pipe and tobacco.

SIR WILLIAM.—Plaid shawl and brooch, stick, bundle of letters. and snuff-box.

MISS GOWER.—Smelling-bottle.

GADD.—Large cigar.

ACT IV

HAND PROPERTIES

Manuscripts and parts for TOM and O'DWYER.

Part for ARTHUR.

Plaid and walking-stick for SIR WILLIAM.

Card for HALL-KEEPER.